# 'THE GOLDEN CROSS LINE'

The Williams brothers; from left to right, Watkin, Robert and Owen. Robert went into banking in Liverpool and was never directly involved in his brothers' shipping ventures. *(Welsh Industrial & Maritime Museum)*

# Owen & Watkin Williams of Cardiff

# 'THE GOLDEN CROSS LINE'

by David Jenkins

Published by the World Ship Society
Kendal LA9 7LT
1991

## CONTENTS

Introduction and Acknowledgements .................................................. 5
Owen & Watkin Williams of Cardiff: The Golden Cross Line ............... 7
Fleet List ........................................................................................ 51
Appendices
    Nomenclature .............................................................................. 61
    Shipping Companies, 1895-1930 .................................................. 62
    Selected Crew Lists ..................................................................... 63
    Sources ....................................................................................... 69
Index of Ships' Names ..................................................................... 70

© **D. Jenkins, 1991**

ISBN 0 905617 61 4

Printed by C.I. Thomas & Sons (Haverfordwest) Ltd., Press Buildings, Merlins Bridge, Haverfordwest, Pembrokeshire.

# INTRODUCTION AND ACKNOWLEDGEMENTS

One aspect of the maritime history of Wales that has fascinated me since I joined the staff of the Welsh Industrial and Maritime Museum in 1982 is the history of the numerous shipping companies founded at Cardiff by natives of the coastal areas of west and north Wales. Of the companies founded at the port by north Walians, that established by the brothers Owen and Watkin Williams in the late 1890s was by far the most prominent, and I have been researching the history of their shipping ventures intermittently for some years. I eventually committed pen to paper in an article that appeared in *Ships Monthly* in February 1990. A draft of this article was read by Mr. Kevin O'Donoghue of the World Ship Society who kindly suggested that an extended version of the article, accompanied by a detailed fleet list, would be acceptable for publication by the Society. This book is the result of that suggestion, and I wish to thank Kevin O'Donoghue for his proposal and also Mr. Robert Shopland, editor of *Ships Monthly,* for allowing me to re-use material that originally appeared in his magazine.

Even a relatively short publication such as this could not have been written without the assistance of numerous individuals. My greatest debt is to Mrs. Iona Roberts, the knowledgeable and ever-helpful historian of Edern and its locality. By providing me with material from her extensive research file she has made my task far easier, and she has also drawn my attention to certain facts and sources of which I would otherwise have been unaware. I have profited greatly from the recollections of Mr. W.P. Williams of Abercynon who was personally acquainted with Owen and Watkin Williams. I also wish to thank the following: Mr. Harold Appleyard, Mr. David Burrell, Mr. Keith Chivers, Mr. Robin Craig, Mr. Aled Eames, Mr. Brian James, Mr. Alfred Jones, Captain Martin Kalnins, Mr. Bard Kolltveit, Mrs. E.C. Llewelyn, Mr. J.L. Loughran, Mr. D.J. Morgan, Captain Gwyn Pari-Huws, Mr. Geraint Phillips, Dr. Dafydd Roberts, Mr. E.N. Taylor, Dr. Huw Walters, Mr. David Williams and Mr. Stewart Williams.

Members of staff of the following companies and institutions have also provided valuable assistance: City of Bristol Museum and Art Gallery, Th. Brovig (shipowners), Farsund, Norway, Cardiff Central Reference Library, Department of Transport Marine Library, London, Furness Withy Group, Glamorgan Archive Service, Cardiff, Guildhall Library, London, Gwynedd Archives Service, Caernarfon and Dolgellau, Hereford Herd Book Society, H.M. Customs & Excise, Cardiff, Latvian Maritime History Archive, Cardiff, Memorial University of Newfoundland, Canada, National Library of Wales, Aberystwyth, National Maritime Museum, London, Public Record Office, Kew, Shire Horse Society and the Welsh Folk Museum.

I acknowledge the cooperation of Mr. Alistair Wilson and Mr. Hywel Rees (respectively Director and Publications Officer of the National Museum of Wales) and Dr. E.S. Owen-Jones, Keeper of the Welsh Industrial and Maritime Museum. My colleagues Dafydd James, Bill Jones and Don Taylor have assisted me with information on various topics in which they specialise, whilst Gordon Hayward has helped with the preparation of many of the photographs included in the book. All the photographs are individually acknowledged, and I am particularly grateful to those members of the World Ship Society who responded to my appeal for additional photographs. The entire text has been typed by Mrs. Carolyn Greene to whom mere thanks seem ridiculously inadequate! I am deeply grateful to everyone who has been of assistance. *Diolch yn fawr iawn i bawb.*

David Jenkins,
Welsh Industrial and Maritime Museum,
Cardiff.

## OWEN & WATKIN WILLIAMS OF CARDIFF: THE GOLDEN CROSS LINE

During the latter half of the nineteenth century, Cardiff was transformed from a modest borough town on the banks of the River Taff to the status of the 'Coal Metropolis of the World'. For a few glorious years prior to 1914, the amount of cargo handled at the port outstripped both London or Liverpool, though unlike the latter ports that handled a wide variety of general cargoes, Cardiff was almost totally dependent upon one export commodity - coal. In 1913, 10½m. tons of 'black diamonds' were exported world-wide from the port, and South Wales was to global energy supplies at that time what the Middle East was to be half a century later. The need for ships to transport this vital source of energy to the four corners of the globe had attracted a number of notable entrepreneurs to Cardiff from the 1870s onwards, and names such as Cory, Morel, Radcliffe, Tatem and Reardon Smith are still synonymous with shipowning at the port, even though none of these companies is involved in shipowning today.

Potential shipowners were attracted to Cardiff from throughout the British Isles and beyond between 1870 and 1914, but remarkably little attention was paid until quite recently to those natives of the coastal areas of west and north Wales who established shipping ventures at the booming coal port. On the eve of the First World War the largest of Cardiff's shipping firms was Evan Thomas, Radcliffe & Co., founded in 1881 by Captain Evan Thomas of Aberporth in Dyfed and Henry Radcliffe, a native of Merthyr Tydfil. Other firms with their roots in west Wales were John Mathias & Sons and Jenkins Brothers. North Wales, however, did not supply Cardiff with as many shipowners. The major port of Liverpool was far closer to the great nurseries of seamen in Llŷn or Anglesey, and shipowners from these areas were significant amongst those operating large fleets of iron and steel sailing vessels from the Merseyside port. Some north Walians nevertheless did establish themselves as shipowners at Cardiff. One of the earliest was Evan Jones who moved from Porthmadog in 1865. By 1880 he was operating three substantial barques, chiefly in the South American trades, and by 1890 he had acquired two steamers. The vast majority of those employed by Evan Jones, both at sea and ashore, were from north Wales, and some time in the early 1880s a young man by the name of Owen Williams joined Jones's office staff as a junior clerk at 10 Bute Dock Esplanade. A native of Edern near Nefyn in the Llŷn Peninsula, he was later to go into partnership with his younger brother Watkin to create one of Cardiff's foremost shipping ventures in the halcyon decades before 1914. Their fascinating and often unusual enterprise is the subject of this short history.

Captain John Williams, Owen and Watkin Williams's father.
*(Gwynedd Archives Service, Henry Parry Collection)*

Owen and Watkin Williams were born in 1862 and 1864 respectively, the second and third sons of Captain John Williams, a native of Porthdinllaen and his wife Mary. Some time between the birth of Owen and Watkin, the family moved to live in a house called 'Tyncoed' in the village of Edern. Like its larger neighbouring village of Nefyn, Edern was a community with an exceptionally strong seafaring tradition. The area's famed herring fishery was well-established as early as the thirteenth century, whilst coastal trading, particularly to Liverpool, developed from the eighteenth century onwards. Large numbers of wooden sailing vessels were built locally and in 1857, aged 36, John Williams became managing owner of one such vessel, the 169 gross ton schooner MARY WATKINS, which he had commanded since she was built at Nefyn in 1850. Despite her relatively small size, the voyages of this vessel, like many other brigs and schooners from north Wales at the time, were wide-ranging. The MARY WATKINS, captained by John Williams and crewed by eight mariners from the Nefyn and Edern locality, carried coal from south Wales, grain from the Black Sea, coffee from Brazil and sugar from the West Indies during the 1860s. In April 1870, the little schooner was at Santos, Brazil when one of the crew members, Watkin Evans, died of the dreaded yellow fever. The £5 wages due to him, together with his personal effects, were eventually returned to his mother, Margery Evans of Porthdinllaen, a sad task for John Williams as Margery Evans was his sister and Watkin had been his nephew.

Captain John Williams sold the MARY WATKINS in 1873 but in 1871 he had bought a 205 gross ton brig, the SHARP, built at Belfast in 1869. Within less than a year of acquiring this vessel, she was lost off the Cape of Good Hope, and local tradition in the Edern area maintained that many of her crew remained in South Africa, finding employment as railway navvies. He went on to acquire, in 1872, the 554 gross ton barque LAURETTA, built at Miramichi in 1865, and in 1875, the substantial 1296 gross ton ship AMOOR, built at Quebec in 1855: they cost respectively, £4,250 and £7,750. Both were typical of the numerous Canadian-built vessels constructed for British owners in the mid-nineteenth century. By this date it would appear that John Williams had retired from active seafaring to concentrate upon the management of his two ships as they traded world-wide. This he continued to do until 1887 when, at the age of 66, he decided to withdraw from shipowning. Both vessels were sold; the AMOOR was bought by the Rev. T. Owen of Porthmadog, only to be abandoned after she ran aground in the River Plate on 1 June 1889, whilst the LAURETTA was ultimately condemned at Valparaiso, though it is not clear when she was broken up.

It can be seen therefore that Owen and Watkin Williams were brought up in an all-pervading atmosphere of seafaring and shipowning, and they must have been familiar from quite an early age with both the practical and commercial aspects of running ships. Owen would appear briefly to have considered going to sea as a means of making a living, but he finally left Edern to join Evan Jones's firm at Cardiff. For Watkin, however, the call of the sea was too strong to be ignored and he served on board his father's ships, narrowly escaping death on one occasion when he fell from the rigging of the AMOOR onto the deck below. Both sons progressed steadily in their chosen careers; by the late 1880s Watkin was First mate on the JENNY OTTO, a 1451 gross ton steamer, owned by G. Otto of London, trading chiefly to the Mediterranean, and in 1889 he joined the well-known Elder, Dempster line as 1st mate of the steamer PALMAS. At the same time, it is clear that Owen was not content with being merely a salaried clerk, as he began to invest in Evan Jones's ships as and when sixty-fourth shares in the vessels became available. In September 1889, for instance, he purchased eight shares in the Jones barque CAROLINE SPOONER from the Rev. John Morgan, who was rector of Edern at that time, and it is likely that his ambition by the early 1890s was to enter into shipowning on his own account.

Owen Williams *(Welsh Industrial & Maritime Museum)*

This ambition was realised on 24 January 1895 when Owen Williams established a single-ship company called simply Hesperides Ltd. to acquire and operate the 2404 gross ton steamer of that name built in 1884 for R.P. Houston & Co. of Liverpool, and designed for their frozen meat trade from the River Plate. The capital of the new firm was £7,000, divided into 140 shares at £50 each; this covered the cost of the HESPERIDES (which was £6,000) and also the cost of her conversion into a conventional dry-cargo vessel. The largest initial shareholder was Owen's uncle, Captain Griffith Owen Williams of Cefnleisiog, Pwllheli, who invested the substantial sum of £1,000 in the vessel on the understanding that he was appointed master, a common arrangement at that time. Owen invested £750, Watkin £500, and one share was taken by their elder brother, Robert, who had entered into the banking profession in Liverpool. Four shares were also taken by the Cardiff chandler Evan Hughes who made minor investments in many Welsh-founded shipping enterprises at Cardiff over the ensuing twenty years, with a view to attracting custom for his business. By May 1895, there were twenty-two shareholders in Hesperides Ltd., amongst whom 104 shares had been

Captain Watkin Williams  *(Welsh Industrial & Maritime Museum)*

allotted in varying proportions. Over the ensuing two years, further individuals acquired shares, including Owen Williams's sisters, Mary and Margery, and Llewelyn Trefan Griffith of Bangor who bought six shares on 1 December 1896 as a condition of his being appointed chief engineer of the HESPERIDES. He was destined to serve Owen and Watkin Williams for over a quarter of a century, later assuming the position of the firm's commodore engineer.

Captain Griffith Williams assumed command of the HESPERIDES on 15 February 1895. It was his first command in steam; up until 1882 he had been master of the AMOOR, but in September that year he assumed command of the iron ship CAMBRIAN MONARCH, owned by

Thomas Williams & Co. of Liverpool. In 1889 he became master of the iron barque METROPOLIS owned by another Liverpool-Welsh company, William Thomas & Co. From 1892 until he joined the HESPERIDES, he also commanded the CROWN OF SCOTLAND, owned by Robertson, Cruikshank & Co. of Liverpool. His first voyage on the HESPERIDES took him to South America on a typical 'coal out, grain home' tramping voyage. There were also similar voyages to the Mediterranean and the Black Sea in 1896, but during the following year the new venture was prematurely terminated when the HESPERIDES became a total loss. On 10 October 1897, she ran aground on the Hatteras Shoal whilst bound from Santiago de Cuba to Baltimore with a cargo of iron ore. All her crew members were saved, but within a fortnight the stranded steamer was hit by a hurricane that reduced her to a tangled, twisted wreck. At the subsequent inquiry Captain Williams was totally exonerated as it was the mate who was on watch at the time, but the loss of the HESPERIDES must have been a considerable blow to his nephew. Owen Williams decided that the best course of action would be to wind the company up voluntarily, which was eventually achieved on 17 January 1898. By this date, he was doubtless already planning his future partnership with Watkin, whose career as a master mariner had also suffered a stroke of bad luck in the mid-1890s.

Having joined Elder, Dempster in 1889, Watkin Williams served as mate on the steamers PALMAS, PLASSEY and MOHAWK before he was appointed master of the MEMPHIS in 1893. The MEMPHIS was one of the vessels employed on Elder, Dempster's Beaver Line trans-Atlantic service, which was eventually acquired by Canadian Pacific in 1903. On 17 November 1896 she was bound from Montreal to Avonmouth, carrying cattle and general cargo when, in dense fog, she ran aground near Mizen Head, Co. Cork. Eleven crew members lost their lives, four being drowned when a lifeboat turned over as it was being lowered. Seven crew members managed to reach the safety of a rock, but five of them were washed off and drowned as the tide rose, and another two drowned whilst trying to reach the rock. The second mate and two engineers were rescued from the foremast rigging by local fishermen. Many of the 350 cattle aboard were drowned, though some managed to break loose to swim ashore near Dunlough.

For many years the story was told in Edern that it was by hanging on to one of these cattle that Watkin Williams had managed to survive the wreck of the MEMPHIS. This story led in turn to his being nicknamed *capten buwch* - the cow captain! As is often the case with a good story, the truth is somewhat more prosaic, though only slightly so, for Watkin was saved by using the wooden door of one of the cattle pens as a raft and paddling himself ashore! The MEMPHIS in the meantime became a total loss, and a report by the Liverpool Salvage Association on 23 November mentioned cheeses, boxes of butter and bacon, deals and dead cattle being washed ashore in the vicinity of the wreck. An inquiry was held at Liverpool on 19 December 1896 as a result of which Watkin Williams had his master's certificate suspended for six months. Despite this, he went on to obtain his extra master's certificate at Liverpool in 1897, but he never again took command of a vessel.

The years around the turn of the century saw the establishment of a number of new shipping enterprises at Cardiff, encouraged by the high freight rates prevailing at the time, largely as a result of the Boer War. It was almost certainly during this period that the two brothers came together to consider the establishment of a partnership at Cardiff, and their combination of commercial and sea-going skills was typical of many shipping ventures in the port at that time. Early in 1898 they ordered a modestly-sized steamer of 940 gross tons from R. Craggs & Sons of Middlesbrough; delivered in September that year at a cost of

The **SILURIAN (1)** of 1898 was the brothers' pioneer vessel.                    (E. N. Taylor)

£13,200, she was named SILURIAN after the prehistoric inhabitants of south-east Wales. To finance the purchase of the vessel, the Silurian Steamship Co. Ltd. was created on 9 August 1898, with a capital of £14,000 divided into 1,400 shares at £10 each. The managers and directors of the new venture were Owen and Watkin Williams, whose offices were at 37 Mountstuart Square, Cardiff. The initial subscribers to the new company were mostly members of the brothers' family who were by that date living at "Pwllparc", Edern, and it is amusing to note that their father John Williams, by then in his seventy-eighth year, described himself as a 'gentleman'.

Shares in the new venture were bought up rapidly; by 16 November that year, 107 shareholders had bought up 1,034 shares. Amongst the earliest investors were the chandler Evan Hughes (who had invested in the HESPERIDES) and the sail and tarpaulin maker Jenkin Jones. A native of New Quay, he had moved his business to Cardiff in 1887 as shipbuilding in his native village declined, and he supplied many Welsh-founded shipping ventures in Cardiff with hatch cloths and awnings. Other investors included Owen and Watkin's elder brother, Robert and his wife Mary, and Dr. Joseph Lister, the Rochdale-born doctor who later lived at Barmouth and had considerable investments in shipping. Over a third of the investors came from Caernarfonshire alone, many from Edern and Nefyn, whilst over two-thirds of the investors were Welsh. This dependence upon capital from their native area and from within the Principality was to be a feature of all the later companies promoted by Owen and Watkin Williams, and that at a time when many Cardiff-based companies were, to an ever-increasing degree, obtaining much of their financial support from the north of England.

At a mere 940 gross tons, the SILURIAN was much smaller than the average size of tramp steamer being ordered by Cardiff owners at the turn of the century. It would appear that the partners' initial intention, however, was not to participate in the traditional 'coal out, grain home' tramping voyages to the Black Sea and the River Plate that were the 'bread and butter' of the Cardiff tramps. They hoped instead to develop a regular line of steamers running outwards to Leghorn (Livorno), Genoa and Marseilles with coal and general cargo, returning with mixed cargoes of fruit and generals from ports on the Spanish Mediterranean coast, where their small steamers could dock with ease. Discharging ports in Britain were to be the well-established general cargo ports of Liverpool and Bristol. Ports such as these were largely free from the clouds of coal dust that shrouded Cardiff, besides which the ports of south Wales had relatively few facilities for the import of general cargoes at that time. In 1900, for instance, Cardiff imported only 338,000 tons of general cargo, whilst coal exports amounted to some 7½m. tons.

Between 1899 and 1901, Owen and Watkin Williams ordered a further seven steamers, all of about 1000 gross tons. The only one built on the Clyde was the 1143 gross ton CANGANIAN, launched from the Govan yard of Mackie & Thomson in December 1899 by Mrs. Grace Griffith, wife of the commodore engineer Llewelyn Griffith. She was followed in 1900 by the DEMETIAN (1108 gross tons) and the ORDOVICIAN (1112

The **DEMETIAN** discharging pitwood at Barrow-in-Furness.
*(Welsh Industrial & Maritime Museum)*

The VENEDOTIAN at Bristol. *(E. N. Taylor)*

gross tons), both built by W. Harkess & Son of Middlesbrough. In 1901, Harkess also supplied the four remaining vessels; the VENEDOTIAN (1168 gross tons), the SEGONTIAN (1171 gross tons), the GOIDELIAN (1220 gross tons) and the CORANIAN (1223 gross tons). The CANGANIAN and all the Harkess-built vessels had long raised quarter-decks, with bridge and engine amidships, but the Craggs-built SILURIAN had a shortened 'three-island' profile with a very tall raked funnel that gave her an endearingly jaunty appearance. All had grey hulls, with brown and white upperworks and yellow funnels, whilst the houseflag consisted of a golden device more similar to a dagger than a cross on a blue background. The pattern of nomenclature initiated with the SILURIAN was continued, and the sometimes obscure derivation of certain names is explained in the relevant appendix.

The construction of this considerable fleet was financed by the flotation of further shipping companies, some owning one vessel, others owning two. The Canganian Steamship Co. Ltd. was established on 7 March 1899 with a capital of £17,000, the Venedotian Steamship Co. Ltd. on 1 September 1900 with a capital of £19,000 and the Segontian Steamship Co. Ltd. on 20 October 1900, again with a capital of £19,000. As was the general practice at that time, these companies were capitalised at, or very near, the purchase price of the vessel to be acquired. Ownership of the DEMETIAN and the ORDOVICIAN was vested in the Steamships Demetian and Ordovician Ltd., set up on 13 October 1899 with a capital of £35,000 in £20 shares, whilst the GOIDELIAN and the CORANIAN were acquired by the Steamships Goidelian and Coranian Ltd. (which had a capital of £40,000) on 6 November 1900. In each case, the vessels were originally acquired from the builder by mortgage, which was paid off as soon as sufficient capital had been raised by the sale of shares in the various companies.

Shares in all but one of these companies cost £10 each and as was the case with the Silurian Steamship Co. Ltd., shareholders from within Wales, and particularly from Caernarfonshire, were particularly prominent. 36 of the 101 shareholders in the Venedotian Steamship Co. Ltd. came from the county, including a number of slate quarrymen such as J.R. Jones of Pentir near Bangor who had invested £50 in the firm, a considerable sum at that time. Similarly, 49 of the 119 shareholders in the Segontian Steamship Co. Ltd. in April 1901 came from Caernarfonshire. Some investors, however, came from further afield. Members of the Harkess family took shares in each of the vessels built at their yard, whilst most of the companies had a small yet significant group of shareholders from the Liverpool, Ormskirk and Southport areas. Were they perhaps business acquaintances of Robert Williams who had been persuaded to buy shares in his brothers' rapidly expanding shipping venture? Of particular interest too were shareholders in the Venedotian and Segontian companies who were employed in various capacities at the Hughesovka Ironworks in the Donetz basin in southern Russia. These works had been established by John Hughes, a native of Merthyr Tydfil who was invited by the Russian authorities to set up an ironworks, chiefly to produce railway lines, in 1869. Due to a lack of skilled labour in Russia at that time, a group of some seventy ironworkers, many of them Welsh, emigrated to work at the new works, and it may be assumed that it was some of these workers, or their descendants, who acquired shares in the VENEDOTIAN and the SEGONTIAN in 1900-01. How they came to acquire these shares must remain something of a mystery, but many single-ship companies founded in Cardiff at that time included a handful of shareholders from Russia.

By 1902 Owen and Watkin Williams had a fleet large enough to maintain weekly outward sailings from either Cardiff or Swansea. Outward cargoes consisted chiefly of coal or patent fuel from either of these ports, supplemented by small parcels of general cargo such as tinplate from Swansea. The ships then generally sailed direct to Leghorn or Genoa where they discharged. Homeward cargoes would then be loaded by inducement at various ports between Marseilles and Gibraltar, and in the Balearic Islands. A close study of the voyage patterns of the vessels during the first decade of the present century reveals that each successive homeward voyage involved calls at a different combination of French and southern Spanish ports. The VENEDOTIAN, for instance, left Swansea on 22 June 1909, arriving at Leghorn on 4 July. Her homeward voyage involved calls at Marseilles and Cartagena before she arrived at Liverpool on 25 July. On other occasions, vessels sailed only to Spanish ports. The CANGANIAN left Cardiff with coal for Aguilas on 10 April 1909; having discharged, she loaded generals for Liverpool at Aguilas and Valencia, sailing from the latter port on 25 April and arriving at Liverpool on 5 May. Thus it can be seen that whilst the brothers' vessels offered regular sailings to the Mediterranean, there were no fixed ports of call on any one voyage, with ships generally calling only at those homeward ports where a cargo was offered.

Owen and Watkin Williams's vessels carried a wide variety of cargo on their homeward voyages. On the evening of 30 September 1909, for instance, the SEGONTIAN was sailing up the Mersey with a cargo loaded chiefly at Valencia, when she collided with the Henderson cargo liner TENASSERIM, outward bound from Birkenhead docks. The SEGONTIAN was beached at Tranmere in a near-sinking condition, and most of her cargo was discharged. Much of it was successfully salvaged and the report on the salvage operation provides a detailed manifest of the vessel's cargo. A considerable proportion of the cargo consisted of marble slabs, strips and chippings, destined for monumental masons throughout Lancashire. Casks of rosin, hemp, coprah oil and salted

The **SEGONTIAN** steaming cautiously up the Avon. *(City of Bristol Museum)*

hides were successfully salvaged, as were cases of castor oil, olive oil and vermouth. The remainder of the cargo consisted of fruit and vegetables; onions, tomatoes, pimentos, melons, raisins and peanuts, most of which, having been thoroughly soaked in the waters of the Mersey, were wisely declared unfit for human consumption! The SEGONTIAN was later dry-docked and repaired, and eventually returned to service on 11 November.

On occasions, additional vessels were chartered by the brothers to maintain their service. One such vessel was the 1442 gross ton Norwegian steamer DAGFIN, which undertook a number of voyages to the Mediterranean from December 1908 onwards. It is also clear that if the opportunity arose and a vessel was available, the brothers were not averse to fixing their vessels on tramping voyages. Ships were occasionally fixed to carry cargoes of coal to Bay ports such as Bordeaux, returning with cargoes of pitwood, and they also loaded homeward cargoes of ores from north African ports and salt from Torrevieja.

The Golden Cross house flag is hoisted as the **GOIDELIAN** arrives at Bristol.
*(City of Bristol Museum)*

Owen and Watkin Williams suffered the first marine losses of their partnership between June 1905 and January 1906. On the evening of 24 June 1905, the GOIDELIAN, commanded by John Daniel Griffith of Edern, was steaming off the southern Portuguese coast, bound for Liverpool with fruit and generals loaded at Valencia and Gandia. The sea was smooth and the weather fine. At about 11.30 p.m. the vessel was off Sagres Point when fog was suddenly encountered. Captain Griffith ordered slow ahead, but ten minutes later there was a tremendous crash as the GOIDELIAN struck rocks below Sagres Point, and then rebounded. An attempt was made to proceed, but it soon became clear that the steamer was sinking. By 2 a.m., there was fifteen feet of water in the engine room and the fires had to be drawn; at 3 a.m. the order to abandon ship was given. No lives were lost, and the crew members were picked up at 10.30 a.m. and later landed at Plymouth. At the subsequent inquiry, Captain Griffith was blamed for not allowing for tidal currents that deflected the GOIDELIAN to the north of her plotted course, and also for failing to use the lead when he had failed to sight the Cape St. Vincent light. His master's certificate was suspended for six months.

As Captain John Daniel Griffith's suspension was coming to an end, his brother Captain Richard Griffith was in command of the ORDOVICIAN, outward bound from Swansea to Genoa with a cargo of patent fuel and generals. Early in the morning of 6 January 1906, the vessel was steaming southwards off the coast of Portugal after a particularly rough crossing of the Bay of Biscay. The sea was still stormy, but it appeared to be clearing so Captain Griffith left the bridge, leaving his mate William Jones in charge with instructions to wake him should the weather deteriorate. What did wake Captain Griffith an hour and a half later was not his mate, but the sound of the ORDOVICIAN running aground on the Portuguese coast at Torres Vedras some twenty miles north of Lisbon. No lives were lost and the entire crew got ashore safely. At the inquiry that followed, the mate William Jones was blamed for the negligent supervision of the crew members on his watch, all of whom were Greeks who spoke very little English. The helmsman had not fully understood the orders given to him by Jones, who in turn had failed to check that the course he had given was being followed at the helm. Jones had his certificate suspended for three months as a result of this incident, and the captain was absolved of all blame.

Two second-hand vessels were acquired later in 1906 to replace these losses. In April, Owen and Watkin Williams bought the Dutch-built 1014 gross ton steamer KINGWOOD from London owners. Renamed CYMRIAN by her new owners, she was only some fifteen months old when she was purchased, at a cost of £16,000. She was followed later that year by a considerably older vessel, the 1969 gross ton steamer SPHEROID, built for Scrutton, Sons & Co. of London in 1891. She was given the name MERVINIAN by Owen and Watkin

The **CYMRIAN** arriving at Bristol.   *(Welsh Industrial & Maritime Museum)*

Williams. On 7 July 1906, ownership of both these vessels was vested in a new shipping company established by Owen and Watkin Williams, The Golden Cross Line Ltd.

The company was described as one that "does not issue any invitation to the public to subscribe for shares", and its entire capital of £15,000 was raised by Owen, Watkin and certain business acquaintances of theirs such as the chandler Owen Hughes (Evan Hughes's son), Captain William Evans, the brothers' marine superintendent and J.R. Palin-Evans who had formerly been a clerk with Owen and Watkin Williams, but who was by then a shipowner himself. It can be seen therefore that whereas the term 'Golden Cross Line' came to be used as a general title for the brothers' cargo service to the Mediterranean, strictly speaking it applied only to this company and its two ships.

The **ARVONIAN** was the first of a number of larger ocean-going tramps acquired by Owen & Watkin Williams from 1905 onwards. *(Welsh Industrial & Maritime Museum)*

A more significant acquisition had been made on 1 September 1905 when the brothers took delivery of the newly-built steamer ARVONIAN from Richardson, Duck & Co. Ltd. of Stockton-on-Tees. She had been launched as ROSEDALE for the Dale Steamship Co. Ltd. of Bristol on 1 August, but was taken over by Owen and Watkin Williams later that month. At 2794 gross tons and capable of loading 5000 deadweight tons on a draft of 22'6", she was clearly far larger than any vessel acquired by the brothers prior to that date and was typical of the ocean-going tramp steamers being operated by Cardiff owners at that time. Moreover, it is clear from her voyages over the ensuing years that she was intended for deep-sea tramping rather than the Mediterranean cargo liner service. In one sense, it was not a particularly auspicious time to enter into tramping because of the prolonged depression in freight rates that lasted from 1903 until 1912, but it did mean that vessels could be obtained quite cheaply from the builders; the ARVONIAN cost £30,550.

A fine study of the **CANGANIAN** arriving at Bristol. *(City of Bristol Museum)*

Owen and Watkin Williams were clearly convinced that carefully managed, up-to-date tramp steamers could be run profitably despite the low freight rates prevailing at the time, for the ARVONIAN was followed by three successively larger vessels; the EDERNIAN (3588 gross tons) in 1906, the SNOWDONIAN (3870 gross tons) in 1907 and the TAVIAN (4567 gross tons) in 1912. The TAVIAN of 1912 was the second vessel of two ordered from Richardson, Duck & Co. Ltd. in 1911-

Captain Evan Williams, Pwllheli, and crew members on board the **ARVONIAN** at an unknown Spanish port, c. 1908. *(Welsh Industrial & Maritime Museum)*

12. By a builder's agreement dated 27 October 1911, however, the contract for the first of these vessels (also intended to be known as TAVIAN) was made over to J.H. Welsford & Co. Ltd. of Liverpool, eventually becoming their INDIANOLA (1912/4566 gross tons). Some confusion attends the transfer of this contract, for it would appear that the vessel was launched on 4 December 1911 as TAVIAN. A little over a fortnight later Welsfords wrote to the well-known ship sale brokers, C.W. Kellock & Co., offering to pay Owen and Watkin Williams £55,000 for the vessel, on condition that the deal was kept "... absolutely private"; this was despite the fact that the brothers had indicated that they were willing to accept the lower sum of £51,500. Despite this confusion, it is certain that the vessel never traded for Owen and

J. H. Welsford's **INDIANOLA** at Emden in 1923.
*(K. J. O'Donoghue collection)*

Watkin Williams and the name was transferred to the second vessel, completed as TAVIAN in December 1912.

No new companies were created to take over the ARVONIAN and the EDERNIAN: the ARVONIAN became the property of Steamships Goidelian and Coranian Ltd. in place of the wrecked GOIDELIAN whilst the EDERNIAN took the place of the lost ORDOVICIAN in Steamships Demetian and Ordovician Ltd. On 30 September 1907, however, Steamship Snowdonian Ltd. was set up with a capital of £35,000 divided into 3,500 shares at £10 each, with the intention of acquiring the steamship SNOWDONIAN, due to be delivered from the builders on 18 October. A lengthy and verbose prospectus published at the time listed the principal features of the new steamer. She was capable of loading 6,700 deadweight tons on a draft of 21'9", which made her ideal for trade to the Plate, the Danube and the Russian Black Sea ports. She had six hatches, all served by double derricks for speedy discharge of cargo, whilst her stokehold was fitted with a steam-powered ash ejector. At £41,750, the prospectus was keen to emphasise that a considerable bargain had been obtained which would repay investors handsomely when freight rates improved once more, as they were certain to do(!) For some reason which is impossible to ascertain, however, Steamship Snowdonian Ltd. was never vested with the ownership of the SNOWDONIAN. The vessel was owned directly by Owen and Watkin Williams until September 1913, when she was transferred to Steamships Goidelian and Coranian Ltd. Steamship Snowdonian Ltd. was wound up on 6 December 1918, and when the TAVIAN was completed in December 1912, she was owned by Owen and Watkin Williams alone, enabling the brothers to profit directly from the good freight rates prevailing at the time.

Most Cardiff tramp steamers at that time tended to stick rigidly to 'coal out, grain home' voyages to the Mediterranean and the River Plate, but the four ocean-going tramps that Owen and Watkin Williams had acquired by 1913 were trading world-wide, carrying a wide variety of cargoes between different ports on voyages that kept them away from the British Isles for extended periods. On 14 February 1912, for instance, the SNOWDONIAN sailed from Cardiff with a cargo of coal for Para in northern Brazil, arriving there on 12 March. She spent almost a month at Para, probably loading timber, before proceeding via Santa Lucia to Baltimore where she arrived on 28 April. On 15 May she sailed for Marseilles with a cargo of grain, and having discharged her cargo, proceeded to Cartagena on 13 June to load ore for Rotterdam. Having discharged her cargo at the Dutch port, she sailed for Cardiff in ballast to load coal once more on 1 July. With only two short ballast legs, this was doubtless a highly profitable voyage, especially as freight rates were improving by 1912 after a very depressed period of almost a decade. On 11 November 1908, Llewelyn Griffith, at that time chief engineer of the SNOWDONIAN, had included the following comment in a letter to his wife, written in the Azores.

". . . I understand the freight market at home is very weak just now. The ARVONIAN went from Barry light to the Gulf of Mexico to load timber for Buenos Aires. . ."

Incredible though it may seem that ships were sailing in ballast from south Wales coal ports in 1908, it is important to note that despite the depressed conditions, Owen and Watkin Williams were determined to keep their ships trading, even if it meant searching out charters at ports all over the world. Many of Cardiff's less enterprising shipowners laid up some of their vessels at this time, but this was clearly not an option that the Williams brothers were willing to consider.

Whilst the larger tramps were steaming across the oceans, seeking cargoes world-wide, the smaller steamers continued to ply back and forth to the Mediterranean. The CORANIAN was sold to Swedish owners in 1907, but a far more serious loss to the fleet was that of the MERVINIAN on 4 October, after barely a year under the Williams brothers' ownership. She was outward bound from Swansea for Marseilles with a cargo of coal and patent fuel when, in very stormy weather, her cargo shifted and she foundered about 100 miles south of the Isles of Scilly. Five lives were lost, including those of the master Captain D. Lewis and a youth who was aboard as a passenger, travelling out to join his father who was the Golden Cross Line agent at Marseilles. During the following year a sister vessel to the CYMRIAN, the 1015 gross ton steamer QUEENWOOD, was acquired and re-named CARDIFFIAN, whilst the VENEDOTIAN was sold to Swedish owners in 1912. A year after her sale, on 6 October 1913, the ARVONIAN was transferred to the ownership of the Venedotian Steamship Co. Ltd.

The **CARDIFFIAN** approaching Bristol Docks. (E. N. Taylor)

It is unfortunate that the records relating to the shipping companies set up by Owen and Watkin Williams that survive in the Defunct Companies files at the Public Record Office give only a very vague indication of their financial performance. Much of the first decade of the present century was characterised by a prolonged depression in freight rates which lasted until 1912, and the balance sheets that have survived from those years often show deficit balances in the profit and loss accounts. Nevertheless, there was no shortage of customers for shares in the various companies, most of which were fully subscribed by 1906. It is also certain that the years leading up to the outbreak of the First World War were highly satisfactory for Owen & Watkin Williams. Freight rates improved considerably, especially in the tramping trades, and their investment in four modern ocean-going tramp steamers, built between 1905 and 1912 when building prices were far lower, doubtless paid handsome dividends during the years 1912-14.

Both Owen and Watkin Williams were bachelors at this time. Owen lived at Plasturton Gardens just off Cathedral Road in Cardiff, but in about 1907 he moved to a small mansion called Hendrescythan between Creigiau and Efail Isaf, some eight miles north-west of Cardiff. Watkin never had a permanent home at Cardiff, but he had a suite of rooms reserved at the Esplanade Hotel on the seafront at Penarth which he used when he was in south Wales. Their father, Captain John Williams, had died in 1899, and the family home at Pwllparc, Edern was kept by their mother Mary Williams and their spinster sisters Mary and Margery. Both brothers would appear to have visited Edern as and when business permitted them to leave Cardiff, and Owen's arrival at Edern in his chauffeur-driven De Dion Bouton car was quite an occasion in the village!

Their Cardiff office at 37 Mountstuart Square was at the commercial heart of Butetown, within easy walking distance of the Coal & Shipping Exchange. It would appear that Owen, having been involved in the commercial aspects of shipping all his working life, was the senior partner in the venture, with Watkin dealing with those matters which he, as a former master, would be more familiar. He had, for instance, superintended the building of all the new steamers built for the firm in 1898-1901. The partners were members of the Cardiff Incorporated Shipowners' Association, though there is evidence to suggest that Owen flirted briefly with the short-lived (1912-14) breakaway Bristol Channel Shipowners' Association. They also acted as Cardiff agents for the Bristol City Line of Steamships Ltd. They ran their firm with a small staff, many of them recruited from the Edern district. Their marine superintendent was their cousin, Captain William Evans, whilst their chartering clerk was John Hughes, Y Wenallt, Edern. However, it was not just their office staff who came from Llŷn, but also a considerable proportion of their seamen. No shipping company can exist without its sea-going staff, and they deserve consideration alongside the firm's principals.

The vessels owned and operated by Owen and Watkin Williams were manned to a considerable degree by officers and seamen from the brothers' native area of Edern and Nefyn, an area with an exceptionally strong seafaring tradition. This tradition, reaching back to medieval times, had developed from the late eighteenth century onwards with the local coasting and slate exporting trades, but by the late nineteenth century, many mariners from the area were going deep sea with the great fleets of sailing ships based at Liverpool. Some of those companies were founded by local men; the 'Castle' line of sailing vessels was founded by Robert Thomas, a native of Nefyn. From Edern too came Captain Hugh Roberts who moved to Newcastle-upon-Tyne in the early 1870s, where he eventually founded the well-known North Shipping Co. Ltd. It can be seen therefore that there was a pool of experienced seamen in the area and it was only natural that Owen and Watkin Williams, amongst other shipowners from the area, should employ men whom they knew and trusted to crew their ships

Between 1895 and 1925 it would appear that no more than some eighteen master mariners were employed on a regular basis by Owen and Watkin Williams. Of those, thirteen were natives of Caernarfonshire, chiefly from Edern and Nefyn; three came from Cardiganshire, whilst two lived at Swansea. Of the latter, Captain C.S. Whyatt, a native of the Forest of Dean, was the only non-Welsh master who served the brothers. What is particularly striking in many cases is the high degree of loyalty that the brothers enjoyed from their captains. This loyalty is well-illustrated in the career of Captain Griffith Roberts, Post Office, Edern. He joined the firm as mate on the SEGONTIAN when new in 1901, and later served as mate on the VENEDOTIAN until he was made captain of

Captain Griffith Roberts, Post Office, Edern. *(Mrs. Iona Roberts, Edern)*

the CORANIAN in 1903. He was then master of the DEMETIAN, VENEDOTIAN and the SEGONTIAN before he was appointed to command the larger EDERNIAN in 1908. He survived the First World War without any hostile incident as master of the SNOWDONIAN and the DEVIAN, and remained with the firm until he left his last command, the motor vessel SILURIAN, on 6 August 1925.

Entire families in the Edern and Nefyn locality came to depend upon Owen and Watkin Williams for employment. The four brothers, Captains

Captain John Daniel Griffith, Edern. *(Gwynedd Archives Service, Henry Parry Collection)*

John Daniel Griffith, Richard Griffith, Thomas Griffith and Griffith Griffith all served with the firm at various times, and John Daniel Griffith went on to become the brothers' marine superintendent following the retirement of Captain William Evans. Similarly the brothers Captains John Williams and Michael Williams also served with Owen and Watkin Williams between 1900 and 1911. Of the three masters from Cardiganshire who commanded the brothers' vessels, the longest serving was Captain D. Alban Thomas of Aberaeron. He was for many years master of the SNOWDONIAN and he named his home in Aberaeron after this ship. There can be little doubt, however, that the best-known of all the masters employed by Owen and Watkin Williams was Captain David John Jones of Swansea. Master of the SEGONTIAN in 1914, he later commanded the MARGRETIAN between 1923 and 1925, but it was after he left Owen and Watkin Williams that he became famous as a Spanish Civil War blockade runner. Nicknamed 'Potato' Jones, his famous comment, ". . . Spanish Navy? Never heard of it since the Armada", endeared him to thousands of people in Britain, and he was accorded the status of a hero in his native Swansea. Official reaction to his swaggering bravado was not so enthusiastic, but there can be little doubt that he had acquired his thorough knowledge of the coast of Spain from his period of service with Owen and Watkin Williams.

As was the case with all Cardiff-owned ships, a proportion of the crew would always be drawn from the ever-changing pool of seamen from all over the world who made Tiger Bay their temporary home. Nevertheless, it is clear from the crew lists (a selection of which are reproduced in the relevant appendix) that there was a close nucleus of Welsh crew members on most of the ships operated by Owen and Watkin Williams. As was the case with the owners, Welsh was the first language of all the locally-recruited crew members who served on their ships, and it was the natural medium of day to day conversation aboard. To the seamen of Edern and Nefyn, Owen and Watkin Williams' ships were *Llongau Pwllparc* - the ships of Pwllparc. There is no reason to believe that conditions on board *Llongau Pwllparc* were any better or any worse than any other ships owned in Cardiff at that time, though it is to the brothers' credit that many of their ships were built with enclosed wheelhouses in an age when such things were considered to be extravagant luxuries by many shipowners. Nevertheless, it cannot be denied that at sea, the hours were long, living conditions sometimes abysmal and the food generally tedious. Some welcome variation in diet was provided by the fact that the ships carried fruit back from the Mediterranean. Whilst serving as chief engineer on the German vessel KARL LEONHARDT, allocated to Owen and Watkin Williams after the war, Llewelyn Griffith mentioned one young crew member who had over-indulged himself:

> ". . .the sailor that acted as watchman in Cardiff - the parson's son - has been laid up this week with chronic diarrhoea. He has been very bad, even passing blood . . . I think he has been eating too many oranges."

Whatever the difficulties of a seafaring life, there can be little doubt that it was made far more bearable for young men from the Edern and Nefyn area by the fact that they were at sea with so many people with whom they were acquainted. This is well captured, again by Llewelyn Griffith, in a letter written by him to his daughter as the crew joined the KARL LEONHARDT at Leith in April 1919:

> ". . . both the second and fourth engineers are here, but the third has not yet arrived. The second is a relative of Capt. Griffith, the one that was on the EDERNIAN, and who came to see you when

we came back from Dieppe. The fourth is an older man than I, and he hails from Edern."

To Llewelyn Griffith, however, the advantages of being at sea with old acquaintances were far outweighed by the disadvantages of separation from his wife and family. There was no formal leave at that time, especially for officers whose services were often retained between voyages. His frustration with being separated from his family, and his worries about being at sea during the First World War are well expressed in a letter written to his daughter from Vladivostok, where the TAVIAN was in port on 10 February 1916:

". . . I hope you had an enjoyable Xmas. I wish I was home as well at the time . . . there is no romance left in sea life; I wish it was over."

An effective antidote to sea fever! Despite the romance attached to seafaring that attracted young men from Llŷn to join shipping compan-

Llewelyn Trefan Griffith, the firm's commodore engineer, in his cabin aboard the **ARVONIAN** in 1907.  *(Captain Gwyn Pari-Huws, Caernarfon)*

ies at Cardiff and Liverpool, there can be little doubt that many of them went to sea because of one basic economic reality: there was no other major form of employment available locally. There were a few granite quarries in the Nefyn district, and most farms employed one or two workmen at that time, but going to sea from the great ports was the only alternative for many young men from the area. Very few of them, however, moved to live in Cardiff or Liverpool; they preferred to retain their homes in their native villages on the Llŷn Peninsula, a fact that in turn maintained the social cohesion of those communities. The sea also offered chances of advancement not available to those who stayed ashore. Able and diligent youths could, with a little good luck, find themselves in command of a ship in their late twenties. The responsibilities that they were expected to shoulder were enormous, and their ability and self-reliance would be severely tested in countless trying situations. At no time were they tested more severely than during the difficult months and years that followed the outbreak of the First World War in August 1914.

The First World War was a period of mixed fortunes for Cardiff's shipowners. Freight rates increased substantially during the first years of the conflict, until unease about war profiteering led to the imposition of Excess Profits Duty in September 1915. This made provision for a duty of 50% to be imposed upon any increase over and above prewar profits, and it was increased to 80% in 1917. The prospect of increased profits was tempered by the German "U-boat" menace. Nine million gross tons of British shipping were to be lost in the conflict as Germany attempted to starve Britain into surrender. Owen and Watkin Williams lost five vessels during the war years, though the first one was to fall victim not to German enemy action but to that old and ever-present adversary, the sea itself. On 13 December 1914, the brothers' pioneer vessel, the SILURIAN, was blown ashore at Angerias whilst bound from Cardiff to Oporto with a cargo of coal; no lives were lost, but the little steamer was damaged beyond repair. Two years later, on 27 December 1916, the CANGANIAN was reported missing with all hands. She was chartered to the Admiralty at the time as a fleet collier, and on 17 November she had sailed from Methil on the Firth of Forth with a cargo of coal for Scapa Flow. She had in fact struck a mine off Montrose on the day she sailed with the loss of her entire crew of eighteen hands.

There were other changes to the fleet beyond those caused by losses. In January 1915, the 3689 gross ton DEVIAN, ordered before the outbreak of war, was delivered by J. Priestman & Co. of Sunderland.

The **MENAPIAN** passing under the Clifton Suspension Bridge. *(E. N. Taylor)*

She was initially owned directly by Owen and Watkin Williams though a 20/64th share in the vessel was later transferred to the Silurian Steamship Co. Ltd. which had been left with no vessel following the loss of the SILURIAN during the previous December. Also acquired in 1915 were two almost identical vessels from Scrutton, Sons & Co. of London. The SARSTOON and the STATIA were both of some 2900 gross tons and dated from 1902; they became MENEVIAN and MENAPIAN respectively under the brothers' ownership. There was one sale that year when CARDIFFIAN was bought by the Llanelli shipowner, William Coombs. She was re-named AFON LLIEDI in accordance with that firm's practice of naming their vessels after rivers in south-west Wales.

In December 1916, all British shipping was brought under government control with the creation of a Ministry of Shipping, headed by the Shipping Controller, Sir Joseph Maclay. The system that had existed since the beginning of the war whereby British merchant vessels were requisitioned as required was ended, and all ships now came under government control at the so-called 'Blue Book' freight rates, which were lower than those pertaining on the open market. Early in the following year, the British merchant fleet began to face the stiffest test of the war as the Germans launched a campaign of unrestricted submarine warfare. Allied shipping losses amounted to over 1 m. gross tons in the spring of 1917, and it was during the summer of that year that Owen and Watkin Williams lost three vessels as a result of enemy action, all within a few weeks of each other. On 2 June 1917 the SNOWDONIAN had evaded a surface attack by a 'U-boat' in the Mediterranean by making smoke, but on 31 July she was captured by U155 some 250 miles south-east of the Azores; her crew was ordered off into the lifeboats and the vessel sunk by explosive charges. Three weeks later the EDERNIAN was torpedoed and sunk six miles south-east of Southwold with the death of fourteen members of her crew, including her master. Ironically, she had only just returned to service having been repaired after striking a mine in the English Channel on 30 March that year. On that occasion she had managed to limp into Dieppe where she was drydocked, but there was to be no second chance for the eleven year-old steamer. Only five days later, the tragedy was compounded with the loss of the CYMRIAN, torpedoed and sunk thirteen miles south-east of the Tuskar Rock, with the loss of ten members of her crew. It was a tremendous blow for Owen and Watkin Williams, but an even greater one for the wives and families of the lost seamen, many of whom had their homes in Edern and Nefyn

It is ironic that only three days after the loss of the CYMRIAN on 25 August, the ARVONIAN was requisitioned by the Royal Navy for conversion to a "Q-ship", one of the apparently innocent merchant ships bristling with armaments that were a significant part of the anti-submarine campaign during the First World War. Initially commissioned as H.M.S. BENDISH, the former ARVONIAN was re-fitted as one of the most heavily-armed 'Q-ships' that saw service in the war. She carried three four-inch guns, three twelve-pounder guns, two machine guns and she had four torpedo tubes fitted, one on each beam, one firing ahead and another firing astern. The four inch guns were concealed behind false lifeboats and hatch covers, and various other disguises were adopted for her other armaments. She operated, without incident, under a number of false names until 26 November 1917 when she was transferred to the United States Navy by arrangement with Admiral W.S. Sims, U.S.N., commanding U.S. naval forces in British waters. Sims was interested in developing the concept of the 'Q-ship' in anti-submarine warfare, and placed the ARVONIAN, which was re-named U.S.S. SANTEE, under the command of Commander D.C. Hanrahan, an experienced American destroyer captain.

The U.S.S. SANTEE's base was to be at Queenstown (Cobh), Ireland and on 27 December 1917 she was steaming towards Bantry Bay on a crew-training exercise, having left base at 4 p.m. At 8.45 p.m. on that cloudy, yet moonlit evening she was struck by a torpedo on her port side, just abaft the engine room bulkhead and about eight feet below the waterline. Despite the fact that the vessel soon had eighteen feet of water in No.4 hold, Hanrahan remained in the area for some two hours with all gun crews at action stations in the hope that the submarine would surface to finish off its victim. No 'U-boat' appeared, however, and Hanrahan reluctantly sent an S.O.S. to Queenstown. With her engineroom and stokehold also flooded, the vessel could raise no steam and had to be towed back to base by the tug PALADIN. Admiral Sims clearly was not impressed with this potential addition to his fleet, for the damaged U.S.S. SANTEE was handed back to the Royal Navy, who had her repaired. She later returned to 'Q-ship' duties, operating from a base at Gibraltar. There can be little doubt that the 'U-boat' commander had recognised U.S.S. SANTEE as a 'Q-ship' for by that stage in the war all German submarine commanders had been issued with handbooks that enabled them to identify tell-tale signs of conversion. It also seems likely that the 'U-boat' had only one torpedo left when she sighted U.S.S. SANTEE, and having fired it, she was unwilling to risk a surface encounter with the heavy armament of the 'Q-ship'. Thanks to this stroke of luck, the former ARVONIAN was to survive the First World War without further incident. The first act in her life story, fascinating and almost incredible as it was later to prove, was over.

Owen and Watkin Williams's fleet was further reduced in 1917 with the sale of the two largest steamers, TAVIAN and DEVIAN to another Welsh-founded Cardiff shipping company, the W. & C.T. Jones Steamship Co. Ltd. Within a year, however, this prominent Cardiff company had withdrawn from shipping altogether, stating that they had very little confidence in the future for tramp shipping. The two years that followed the cessation of hostilities in November 1918 constituted a period of unprecedented upheaval in the history of shipowning at Cardiff. The end of the war signalled the beginning of a fantastic shipping boom, based largely on the false assumption that there was a shortage of tonnage as a result of war losses. The apparent shortage was in fact caused largely by extreme post-war dislocation at many ports that led to congestion and delays. The illusion of a shortage of tonnage thus created was soon reflected in spiralling freight rates and tonnage prices. Newcomers, who had little or no experience of shipping's potentially extreme fluctuations, rushed headlong into the industry, buying up all manner of tonnage at grossly inflated prices. Cardiff's older-established shipowners viewed this great jamboree with detached realism, doubting whether the boom would last, but nevertheless willing to sell off most, or even all of their fleets and making handsome profits in the process. In addition to W. & C.T. Jones, a number of other well-known firms sold up at this time. John Mathias & Sons had disposed of their last vessel by 1922, whereas Evan Jones & Co., with whom Owen Williams had started his career forty years previously, never bothered to start rebuilding their fleet after war losses had left them without ships by 1918.

Uneasy at what he too felt to be a period of commercial madness, Watkin Williams decided to withdraw from the managing partnership during 1919 and he retired to live with his mother and sisters in Edern. Owen remained in business, however, operating from new offices in Baltic House to which the firm had moved in May 1916. There can be little doubt that he did very well out of the brief flourish of prosperity that lasted from January 1919 until May 1920. The various shipping companies that were under his management had emerged from the war in exceptionally strong financial circumstances. Considerable sums had been paid by the government as compensation for losses; Steamships Goidelian & Coranian Ltd., for instance, had received £115,375 after the loss of the SNOWDONIAN. Owen shunned the temptation to acquire additional tonnage, but disposed of two vessels at good prices. The SEGONTIAN was sold for £22,500 on 18 December 1919, whilst the DEMETIAN was disposed of at a similar price a month later. Added to this substantial income from ship sales was the equally healthy income being generated by those vessels still trading on a boom market. Between October and December 1919, for instance, the MENAPIAN and the MENEVIAN showed a net profit in excess of £18,000 on their voyages to the Mediterranean.

Though Owen Williams had sold two vessels in 1919-20, the strength of his fleet was upheld by the allocation in April 1919 of three German vessels surrendered to the British after the war. They were the 1868 gross ton JENNY, built in 1904, the 3129 gross ton KARL LEONHARDT of the same age and the older ROMA, a 2606 gross ton steamer built in 1889. Llewelyn Griffith was appointed chief engineer of the KARL LEONHARDT which he joined at Leith on 23 April 1919. He later wrote of his new charge,

". . . she is not likely to be a greyhound,"

but writing from Buenos Aires in September, he was obviously becoming quite fond of the ex-German steamer:

". . . KARL has been painted slate colour outside and funnel yellow - company colours. She is quite a swank now and 'camouflaged' like this she has the impression that the world would not think her to be German anymore!"

All three vessels remained under Owen Williams's management until 1921, when they were sold to various shipowners. The JENNY remained with Cardiff owners as D.P. Barnett's PENTAFF until 1926, whilst KARL LEONHARDT was sold to the Greek Government and the ROMA returned to Germany, acquired by a firm from Stettin.

There can be little doubt that by the latter years of the war, Owen Williams was a man of considerable wealth. He had married on 12 June 1917, at the age of 55, Margaret, the 17-year old daughter of Mr. Daniel P. Thomas of Llanilltud Faerdref, a mining engineer and manager of the Pwllgwaun Colliery which formerly stood on the present site of Pontypridd Rugby Football Club's ground at Sardis Road, Pontypridd. Due to the appalling conditions that prevailed underground at this pit, it was known as 'Dan's Muck Hole', but this did not prevent Owen

'Dan's Muck Hole'; the Pwllgwaun Colliery at Pontypridd, owned by Owen Williams from 1917 until 1924.   *(Welsh Industrial & Maritime Museum)*

Williams from buying the pit and putting his new father-in-law in full control of the operations there. Owen also invested much of his wealth in the acquisition of landed estates. As a bridal home he bought a substantial house called Crossways near Cowbridge (which he later extended), together with the Rayer and Nash estates, totalling some 2,700 acres in the fertile Vale of Glamorgan. Both Owen and Watkin were interested in agriculture, and their sisters farmed the land at Pwllparc on a modest scale. There was nothing modest, however, about Owen Williams's entry into farming on his new estates. He joined the Shire Horse Society in 1917, buying a number of pedigree mares and fillies, and in September 1918 he paid 250 guineas (a record price) for a filly which he named 'Crossways Forest Maid'. In 1922 and 1923 she was champion mare at the Shire Horse Society's London Show, and she was also champion in her class at the Royal Welsh Show in 1923. Owen also began to breed Hereford cattle and again paid record

Crossways House, Cowbridge, purchased by Owen Williams in 1917.
*(Stewart Williams, Barry)*

prices (£2,200 for one heifer) at a notable sale held at Pembridge in 1918. His purchases, both of horses and cattle, aroused considerable comment, chiefly because of the vast sums that he had paid at a time when pedigree livestock prices were as inflated as those prevailing in shipping.

'Crossways Forest Maid', Owen Williams's Shire mare that was the Shire Horse Society's Champion Mare in 1922 and 1923. *(Keith Chivers, Shire Horse Society)*

Cardiff's great post-war boom came to an end during the latter half of 1920. From May onwards freight rates began to tumble as the shipping market realised that there was no shortage of tonnage, but rather an excess. By December 1920 freight rates were in some cases less than a quarter of those prevailing twelve months previously. Many of Cardiff's newer shipowners, unable to pay for vessels recently acquired at grossly inflated prices, found themselves in severe financial straits. Ships were sold for a sixth of the price paid for them only a few months before and the newspapers of the period were full of reports of the collapse of dozens of companies established during those euphoric eighteen months in 1919 and 1920. Having distanced himself from the worst excesses of the boom, Owen Williams was better placed to face the future than many, but the effects of the low freight rates were soon to be felt throughout Cardiff's shipping circles. Owen's intention was to rebuild the Golden Cross Line service after the disruption of the war years and by 1921 he had re-established a monthly service with the MENAPIAN and the MENEVIAN. He was also, however, about to embark upon a daring shipping innovation, albeit one that would eventually play a major part in his eventual demise as a shipowner.

The first successful ocean-going motor vessel was the SELANDIA, completed by Burmeister & Wain of Copenhagen in 1912 for the well-known Danish East-Asiatic Line. In the early 1920s a number of British firms such as Silver Line and Walter Runciman's Moor Line were to acquire motor vessels, but many shipowners, particularly at Cardiff, were sceptical of the value of the new form of propulsion. The triple-expansion steam engine was cheaper to build, easier to maintain and caused much less vibration than the early diesels. Motor vessels might be cheaper to crew and more convenient to bunker, but most Cardiff shipowners were wary about introducing such vessels to a port that owed its very existence to the export of high quality steam coal. Owen Williams was apparently convinced, however, that the future lay with the motor vessel, and it may be significant that another liner company operating to the western Mediterranean, MacAndrews, had acquired their first such ship, the 1365 gross ton PINZON, in January 1922. Later that year Owen placed an order with Charles Hill & Sons of Bristol for the construction of a twin screw motor vessel of 2578 gross tons, the first motor vessel ever ordered by a Cardiff owner. She was to be powered by two Beardmore-Speedwell hot bulb semi-diesel engines built by William Beardmore & Co. of Glasgow. Each engine had six cylinders, producing 600 b.h.p. at 185 r.p.m. , and it was claimed that the advantages of this particular design were low cost, relatively light weight and economic fuel consumption. She was a five-hatch shelter decked vessel with engines aft and bridge house amidships, though she was not very handsome, with an ungainly cruiser stern and a squat funnel.

The vessel was launched by Mrs. Margaret Williams on 15 May 1923, having been christened MARGRETIAN after her sponsor. A considerable amount of attention was lavished on the new ship by the maritime press, and the journal *The Motor Ship* ran a number of articles about the vessel and her engines. At about this time, Owen Williams also ordered a second, though much larger motor vessel of almost 7000 gross tons, to be built by the Blythswood Shipbuilding Co. Ltd. of Glasgow for delivery late in 1924. This vessel was to be fitted with Italian-designed six-cylinder Tosi diesel engines, built under licence by Beardmore and capable of producing 1750 b.h.p. at 130 r.p.m. She was to be named SILURIAN, after the brothers' pioneer steamer built in 1898.

The ill-fated **MARGRETIAN**, shortly after her completion in 1923.
(E. N. Taylor)

The financial outlay on these two new vessels was enormous; the MARGRETIAN alone, delivered in November 1923, cost £140,000. Meanwhile freight rates had not recovered after the crash of 1920, and the MENAPIAN and the MENEVIAN were running up mounting losses on the Golden Cross Line service. Whereas coal had always been available as an outward cargo prior to 1914, the terms of the Versailles agreement soon flooded Europe with cheap German reparations coal. Coal exports from south Wales to Italy fell from almost 5 m. tons in 1913 to 2.8 m. tons in 1925. Thus the vessels often sailed outwards with just a few parcels of general cargo, with one outward voyage by the MENEVIAN in 1921 earning the miserable freight of £363-7-10d, as opposed to a freight of over £3,500 which could be obtained for an outward cargo of some 4,000 tons of coal from Barry to Genoa at that time. Between August 1920 and November 1921 the MENAPIAN and MENEVIAN made a joint trading loss of almost £30,000. Further complications had arisen with regard to the sale of the SEGONTIAN in 1919 to the Lyndon Steamship Co. Ltd. of Cardiff, established at the height of the boom in June 1919. A sale price of £22,500 had been agreed, but being unable to pay the sum outright, it had been agreed that the Lyndon Steamship Co. Ltd. would take the vessel on a mortgage from Owen Williams. This appeared to be a perfectly satisfactory arrangement in 1919 when freight rates were high, but two years later, with rates having slumped, only £2,500 had been repaid.

Owen Williams had also advanced a sum of money to another of the companies set up in the boom, the Brynllwyd Shipping Co. Ltd. This firm was floated in April 1920 by William Morgan and his son Idris. William Morgan had started work as a clerk with Evan Jones & Co. a few years after Owen Williams, but had remained with the company until its demise after the First World War. In partnership with his son he had then decided to establish the Brynllwyd Shipping Co. Ltd. to acquire the 375 gross ton coaster MARENA, dating from 1908. He then approached his former colleague in the hope of arranging a loan to buy the MARENA, and in May 1920, Owen Williams advanced Morgan the sum of £26,100, secured by a mortgage on the coaster. The new company had a capital of £30,000 in £1 shares, though by the end of 1920 less than £8,000 had been raised by the sale of shares and serious financial difficulties were foreseen unless freight rates improved. By 1923 therefore, not only did Owen Williams have to contend with the problems being faced by his own shipping enterprise as a result of the low freight rates; he had also made two substantial loans to shipping companies established during the false optimism of the post-war boom whose financial prospects were less than promising.

It was Owen Williams's hope that the motor ships, once they were trading, would be able to offset these losses, but his hopes were to be cruelly dashed, particularly in the case of the MARGRETIAN. In his choice of machinery for this vessel he had been unfortunate in adopting an untried make of questionable reliability; the engines failed to live up to their manufacturer's claims and were plagued with continuous breakdowns that badly disrupted the Golden Cross Line services throughout 1924. Owen attempted to sue Beardmores, but after lengthy litigation only succeeded in getting compensation amounting to the paltry sum of £12,500. At the same time, a considerable sum was being spent on improvements to the MENAPIAN and the MENEVIAN, both of which were by then over twenty years old. Between January 1924 and September 1925 some £71,000 was spent on general repairs and the conversion of both vessels to oil firing. This considerable outlay can have done nothing to ease the growing debt of the entire enterprise, added to which the two steamers had sustained a loss of over £24,000 on their trading in 1924.

The fleet was augmented in November 1924 with the delivery of the second motor vessel, SILURIAN. *The Motor Ship* reported the predelivery trials of the vessel on the Clyde earlier that month in glowing terms, describing her as the largest ocean-going single-deck motor cargo vessel yet built. Capable of loading 11,000 tons, with a service speed of 11 knots and equipped with all-electric auxiliaries, she was certainly an impressive vessel, and a noteworthy predecessor of today's bulk carriers, but one wonders what Owen Williams's true feelings were that day as he surveyed the Clyde from the SILURIAN's bridge, accompanied by interested representatives from such prominent British shipping companies as the Ellerman City Line and Shaw, Savill & Albion. 1924 had been a disastrous year for him. In order to offset the mounting losses of his shipping enterprise, he had been forced to sell off his estates in the Vale of Glamorgan earlier that year, whilst he sold Pwllgwaun Colliery to his father-in-law. Also sold were his Shire Horse stud and his herd of pedigree Herefords, both of which had proved disastrous financially. The breeding cows had been stricken with an aborting disease which meant that there were no calves produced for sale to other breeders, whilst livestock prices in general had crashed by the time of the sales. A three year old heifer, whose grand-dam cost Owen Williams £2,000 in 1918, was sold for £75 in the sale held on 3 October. The Shire stud too sold for a fraction of the price paid in the latter years of the war; the post-war glut of horses and a surge in farm mechanisation had caused prices to plummet so far that horses were often unsaleable.

He was also beset by emotional problems. On 31 March 1924 he had been forced to foreclose on his mortgage to the Brynllwyd Shipping Co. Ltd., thus ending the brief shipowning career of his friend and former colleague William Morgan. Worse still, his marriage was breaking up. He was utterly devoted to his young wife and had lavished her with gifts. It is said that on her birthday in 1921 the MENEVIAN arrived at Cardiff from the Mediterranean with a large object covered with white canvas on her No.1 hatch. Owen took his wife down to the docks to watch the vessel's arrival, and as the MENEVIAN was made fast, the canvas was drawn away to reveal a gleaming Fiat sports car! By 1924, however, Margaret Williams's liaison with a prominent Indian cricketer and nobleman had led to their separation. A dispersal sale was held at Crossways in December 1924. Shortly before the sale, an antiques expert, J. Kyrle Fletcher visited the mansion, and he later wrote an article for the *Western Mail* describing its contents. He was amazed at both the quantity and quality of what he saw: a room furnished entirely with eighteenth century French furniture, walls hung with early Flemish tapestries, fine silverware from the Tudor and Stuart periods and a collection of the very best Welsh porcelain from the Swansea and

The magnificent drawing room at Crossways, Owen Williams's home near Cowbridge.
*(Welsh Folk Museum)*

Nantgarw potteries. The article was a poignant testimony to the fine lifestyle enjoyed by Owen Williams and his wife during their brief marriage, but times had changed - and so had Owen's luck.

It would appear that much of the capital acquired by Owen Williams from the sale of his estates was used to provide loans to the various shipping companies in an attempt to keep them solvent. A personal loan of over £16,000 was made to the Segontian Steamship Co. Ltd., whilst an even greater loan of over £21,000 was made to Steamships Goidelian and Coranian Ltd. As can be seen from the relevant appendix, the SILURIAN was owned outright by Owen and Watkin Williams, but the MARGRETIAN and the two steamers belonged, in varying proportions of 64th shares, to combinations of the surviving single-ship companies. It is difficult to see what advantage, if any, was gained from these arrangements. The entire situation was clearly far from satisfactory and matters eventually reached a crisis in 1925. With freight rates still low, Owen Williams realised that he could no longer go on sustaining such tremendous losses, and in June 1925 the MARGRETIAN was laid up on the mud near Cardiff's Pierhead. The other vessels were laid

A view from the Pierhead, Cardiff, c. 1926. As the Campbell steamers come and go, the **MARGRETIAN** is laid up in the background. *(National Maritime Museum)*

up in October that year, and the MENAPIAN and the MENEVIAN were sold shortly afterwards, both vessels together fetching a mere £17,475. The SILURIAN was sold to Furness Withy & Co. in 1927 (after an interesting episode in which Captain Griffith Roberts had been ordered to sail her to Hamburg to avoid arrest for debt at a British port), whilst the MARGRETIAN, having lain on the mud for over three years, was sold in November 1928 for £9,650. This sum was approximately one fourteenth of her cost to the firm when new in 1923. In all, debts of almost £½ m. had been incurred between 1923 and 1928 and such was the personal strain imposed by the whole affair that Owen Williams suffered a severe breakdown in health. On reflection, this is hardly surprising. In the space of eighteen months from January 1924, he had lost everything - his wife, his home, his estates, his much-prized livestock and the shipping line which had been his life's work. He left Cardiff and took a suite of rooms at a London hotel where he lived a semi-reclusive life for some years before deciding in 1930 to wind up the various shipping companies still in existence.

The winding-up of the companies in April 1930 was a mere formality. Two of the companies, the Silurian Steamship Co. Ltd. and the Canganian Steamship Co. Ltd. had been voluntarily liquidated in 1917 when the shareholders got a good return on their investments. This was not to be the case in 1930 as the companies were all insolvent and there was no capital left to distribute amongst the investors. In reports to shareholders in the remaining five companies liquidated in 1930, the Cardiff accountants W.R. Gresty & Co. stated that in each case there had been a total loss of the whole of the shareholders' capital, and of the reserves that had formerly existed. Due to the way in which ownership of the MARGRETIAN, MENAPIAN and MENEVIAN had been divided amongst four of the remaining companies, the accountants had found it complicated to calculate the individual debt of each company, but at the final reckoning there was an overall deficit balance of £428,587. As of 16 May 1930, the shipping venture commenced by Owen and Watkin Williams thirty-two years earlier ceased to exist.

The Golden Cross Line Ltd., established by Owen and Watkin Williams on 9 July 1906 was wound up along with the other companies on 16 May 1930, but the cargo service established by the brothers survived, having been taken over in the late autumn of 1925 by Lambert, Barnett & Co. of Cardiff. Their fleet of seven steamers ran a monthly service to Genoa, Leghorn, Marseilles and southern Spain, chiefly from Cardiff and Swansea. By 1935, D.P. Barnett had established a successor company called the Golden Cross Line (Bristol Channel) Ltd. which owned the 1988 gross ton steamer PENTHAMES. This vessel was sold to the

D. P. Barnett's steamer **PENTHAMES** at Cardiff in 1936. Note the Golden Cross device on both funnel and houseflag. *(Welsh Industrial & Maritime Museum)*

Ulster Steamship Co. Ltd., Belfast in 1937. During the Spanish Civil War, Barnett was managing a fleet of up to fourteen vessels, most of which were at various times engaged upon the risky, yet highly profitable business of running Franco's blockade. The war obviously disrupted the regular Golden Cross Line service, though chartered vessels sometimes took on cargoes. In May 1937, for instance, the Abbey Line's NEATH ABBEY loaded fruit for the Golden Cross Line at Valencia, Castellon and Burriana bound for Liverpool. By 1942, the company managed the EMPIRE PLANET on behalf of the Ministry of War Transport. This vessel was transferred to Swansea registry in 1943 and eventually sold in 1946.

In January 1946, the share capital of the Golden Cross Line (Bristol Channel) Ltd. was jointly acquired by Charles Hill & Sons, managers of the Bristol City Line, and Turnbull Scott & Co. Ltd. of London. For some seven months during 1951, the 6140 gross ton LONDON CITY was registered in the name of the Golden Cross Line. In 1952 the line was sold yet again, to Harris & Dixon of London, who operated a service to the Mediterranean with their 942 gross ton motor vessel GRACECHURCH, and they eventually altered the name of the service to the Gracechurch Line. In 1959 the rights of the Gracechurch Line were acquired by Constantine Lines Ltd. of Middlesbrough, and later by Anthony & Bainbridge Ltd. of Newcastle-upon-Tyne. The line is still in existence today, operating a container service to the Mediterranean with chartered tonnage. The chief ports served in the British Isles are Liverpool and, as of August 1988, Swansea, so that the present service is very similar indeed to that initiated by Owen and Watkin Williams at the turn of the century. The Golden Cross Line too remains in existence. Its share capital was acquired by Manchester Liners Ltd. on 29 November 1968 to expand the company's interests in the Mediterranean trades and it presently exists as a dormant company within the Furness Withy Group.

A few of the vessels built originally for Owen and Watkin Williams enjoyed remarkably long and in some cases, very eventful lives. The SEGONTIAN survived until 1956 under Swedish ownership whilst the

The **BALLA** (ex-MARGRETIAN); between 1937 and 1961 she was owned by the Norwegian shipowner Th. Brovig of Farsund. *(Th. Brovig, Farsund, Norway)*

**SPIDOLA** (ex-ARVONIAN) amidst the Baltic ice.          *(Latvian Maritime History Archive)*

CORANIAN remained in service until 1968 as the Turkish-owned ILHAN. The MARGRETIAN was sold in 1928 to Stewart & Esplen of London and was re-engined with two ex-'U-boat' engines in 1930 when she was transferred to the Gresham Shipping Co. Ltd. of London. Having traded for only two years, she was laid up at Blyth, but in August 1936 she sailed for West Africa, only to break down off Portugal. She was then towed into Lisbon. In 1937 she was sold to the Norwegian shipowner Th. Brovig of Farsund, who re-named her BALLA and employed her on their Yucatan Line service from New Orleans and Houston to Mexican ports. Clearly her replacement German engines were only a little more reliable than those originally fitted by Beardmores and on one occasion in 1941, en route for Houston, she ran out of fuel. A jury rig using hatch cloths was hurriedly improvised, and with a following wind she achieved seven knots, only fractionally slower than if she had been under power! In 1948, Brovig re-fitted her with two American-built diesel engines driving a single screw, and she remained with the Norwegian company until 1961 when she was sold to a Mexican shipping firm and re-named GUADALAJARA. Her fate is uncertain, but she was probably broken up in 1969.

By far the most remarkable story, however, is that of the ARVONIAN. In 1919 she was sold to the Rhondda Shipping & Coal Exporting Co. Ltd., Cardiff who re-named her BROOKVALE. Eight years later she was sold to the Latvian shipowner Peter Dannebergs of Riga and re-named SPIDOLA. For twelve years she operated as a typical Baltic tramp, carrying timber outwards to a variety of destinations and returning with coal from the Tyne and iron ore from North Africa. In October 1939, with Europe descending into the abyss of war, she sailed from Riga in ballast to load coal at Dunston for Sweden. Though a neutral ship, she was intercepted by a German patrol boat on 26 October and eventually escorted into Kiel where her master was thoroughly interrogated as to the nature of the voyage. It is likely that the Germans recognised her as a former 'Q-ship', and were suspicious that her owners wished to hand her over to Britain for similar use in the Second World War, but the SPIDOLA was eventually released on 3 November.

After failing to fulfil her charter, the SPIDOLA returned to the Baltic to load pitwood for Belgium. Having arrived at Kiel with a full cargo for Antwerp on 26 December, she was once again impounded under new German rules regarding the export of raw materials to Holland and Belgium! Later escorted to Hamburg, she was forced to discharge her cargo on 9 April 1940, and was not released until 25 May. On both occasions no compensation was paid for loss of earnings, though upon her release she was allowed to load coal for Riga at Nordenham. Soon afterwards, on 17 June 1940, the Red Army invaded Latvia and annexed the republic to the U.S.S.R. On 22 July 1940 decrees were passed providing for the nationalisation of all private companies and by August 1940 the SPIDOLA was flying the Soviet flag following the total incorporation of Latvia by Russia. Almost a year later, with Hitler's armies sweeping into Russia, the SPIDOLA was in dry dock at Liepaja. On 30 June she was taken as a prize by the Germans; re-named RUDAU, she was eventually allocated to the German Navy, managed by Schulte & Bruns of Emden. Placed in service as a troop transport and supply vessel sailing chiefly between Germany and Norway, she survived collision with a submerged wreck in Greifswald Bay and an aerial attack by the R.A.F. Following the liberation of Europe, she was taken over by the Allied Shipping Commission and used to re-patriate German prisoners of war from Norway until laid-up at Kiel in 1946.

On 15 April 1947 the RUDAU, together with six other ex-Latvian ships, was taken over by the Ministry of Transport, and having been manned by a crew of displaced Latvian seamen, she sailed for London with a cargo of timber. At London she was placed under the Red Ensign, re-named SPIDOLA and once more found herself managed by a Welsh shipping company, Richard W. Jones & Co. of Newport. Still crewed by Latvians, who kept the old steamer in immaculate condition, she survived a serious grounding off Holy Island, Anglesey, on 14 February 1948. She was operated in the intermediate tramp trades until 1952 when she was returned to her rightful owner, Mrs. Velta Neimans (the daughter of the late Peter Dannebergs) who was by then living in Costa Rica. The SPIDOLA was re-registered under the Costa Rican flag at Puerto Limon and traded for a further six years until she was sold to Walter Ritscher & Co. , Hamburg in 1958 and broken up later that year. Having survived shipwreck, torpedoes, bombs and aerial attack, the former ARVONIAN finally succumbed to the scrapman's torch, though her longevity was a splendid tribute to the quality of craftsmanship at the Tees-side yard where she was built. It was an ignominious end to a remarkable tramp steamer whose career both encompassed and reflected over fifty stormy years of European history.

Owen Williams eventually returned to live with his family at Pwllparc, Edern. Watkin had made it his home since he retired from the partnership in 1919 and three years later he purchased the freehold of the property from the Llanfair estate and carried out a number of alterations.

Pwllparc, Edern, 23 May 1989. *(Author)*

At first sight Pwllparc is no different from dozens of other solidly-constructed farmhouses that dot the beautiful Llŷn Peninsula, but closer inspection reveals a number of fine features that show it to have been the home of a relatively wealthy family. It is approached along a short conifer-lined drive, at the end of which, alongside the house, stands a substantial garage that clearly dates from a period when few people in Edern would have owned a car. Many of the windows in Pwllparc have attractive stained glass inserts portraying maritime scenes, whilst a pleasant conservatory was added to the front of the house, facing south to enjoy the sun all day. In front of the house are neat lawns and gravel paths, whilst a modest brick-walled garden with greenhouses is to be found nearby. In all, the house is an apt reflection of the brothers' background, much more so than the vanished splendour of the Esplanade Hotel, Penarth, or the rambling grandeur of Crossways.

Mrs. Mary Williams, the brothers' mother, died in 1931, aged 97. During her long life she had seen the rise and fall of both her husband's and her sons' shipping ventures, and was probably, through hard experience, only too aware of the considerable risks taken by anyone venturing into shipping. At the time of her death, Watkin held the post of High Sheriff of Caernarfonshire, certainly the most elevated of the numerous public offices that he held after returning to his native area.

Watkin Williams in his dress as High Sheriff of Caernarfonshire, 1930-31.
*(Welsh Industrial & Maritime Museum)*

He was also a Justice of the Peace and a member of the Llŷn Rural District Council, but he was particularly keen in his support of the R.N.L.I. and was chairman of its South Caernarfonshire branch for many years. All the family were faithful members of the Calvinistic Methodist chapel at Edern, and both Owen and Watkin, like Hugh Roberts, Newcastle, before them, had been generous in their financial support of the cause.

Owen Williams died at Pwllparc on 26 May 1938 aged 75; the impact of the financial disaster that overwhelmed him in the 1920s is starkly reflected in the fact that his entire estate was valued at a nominal £5. Watkin, who never married, died six years later on 11 August 1944, leaving £67,500, a sum that reflected the wisdom of his decision to get out of the managing partnership in 1919. Nevertheless, he must have lost a good deal of money when the shipping venture finally collapsed for he had retained his shares in all the surviving shipping companies managed by his brother. Both brothers lie buried with their parents and their spinster sisters in the chapel graveyard at Edern, only a few yards from the grave of Hugh Roberts and his wife. The only member of the family not buried at Edern was the eldest son Robert, who outlived both his brothers, dying at his retirement home at Deganwy in 1950. One of his daughters, Miss Mary Eames Williams later bequeathed a sum of money to the R.N.L.I. which enabled the Institution to build a new Watson-class lifeboat for the Moelfre station on Anglesey in 1956. Named WATKIN WILLIAMS in recognition of her namesake's association with the R.N.L.I., this was the lifeboat with which Coxswain Richard

Coxswain Richard Evans, Moelfre with his former lifeboat **WATKIN WILLIAMS** on the occasion of the vessel's purchase by the Welsh Industrial & Maritime Museum, 7 June, 1983. *(Welsh Industrial & Maritime Museum)*

Evans of Moelfre rescued crew members from the Greek motor vessel NAFSIPOROS in 100-knot winds on 2 December 1966. Richard Evans received his second R.N.L.I. gold medal in recognition of his exceptional achievement. Transferred from Moelfre in 1977, the WATKIN WILLIAMS saw service at Oban, but was finally withdrawn in 1983 and purchased by the Welsh Industrial and Maritime Museum. Here at Cardiff she will remain, not only as a tribute to the bravery of Richard Evans but also as a memorial to Watkin Williams, who knew from bitter experience what it meant to be shipwrecked.

During his retirement years Robert Williams was interviewed by David Thomas, the pioneer of modern writing on Welsh maritime history. Robert, who had of course been a banker all his working life, was of the opinion that the people of Llŷn should not have invested their money in ships. He was speaking in 1926 when it was becoming clear that those who held shares in the various remaining shipping companies established by his brothers had lost virtually everything that they had invested. Many shareholders in the late 1920s must have regretted bitterly the day when they "cast their bread upon the waters", but in their anxiety at that time it was perhaps easy for many of them to forget the many good years of trading enjoyed by Owen and Watkin Williams from which they in turn had profited. In its report on the final winding-up of the companies published on 27 March 1930, the *Western Mail* emphasised that the brothers' shipping ventures had ". . . carried on successfully over a long period of years", and the extent of the financial disaster that had overwhelmed Owen Williams was reported almost with disbelief.

This was hardly surprising. Despite the depressed freight rates prevailing between 1903 and 1912, it is likely that, taken overall, the period from the foundation of the brothers' venture in 1898 up until 1914 was generally successful. The fact that Owen and Watkin Williams operated a diverse shipping venture, that comprised both the Golden Cross Line service to the Mediterranean and, by 1913, a fleet of four modern tramp steamers trading world-wide, probably made the entire enterprise less susceptible to variations in the freight market. They were certainly more enterprising in the operation of their tramps than many Cardiff owners, not being content to participate in the 'coal out, grain home' trade alone, but also seeking out cargoes and charters world-wide during the depression of 1903-12. The difficult years of the First World War also brought with them improved profits, though at the same time the brothers adopted a cautious policy, with most of the companies under their control committing sums of up to £10,000 *per annum* to reserves against depreciation. Caution was also the keynote of policy during the boom of 1919-20, with Owen Williams selling older tonnage and resisting the temptation to acquire new vessels at grossly inflated prices. By 1920, Owen had been long enough in the shipping business to know that it was particularly susceptible to violent financial fluctuations, and his success up until then reflected the experience that he had gained in over forty years in the industry.

What therefore brought about the downfall of this apparently well-founded enterprise? One significant factor was Owen Williams's prodigal spending on houses, landed estates, pedigree livestock and a colliery between 1917 and 1920, which contrasts sharply with his more cautious policy with regard to shipping during those years. All these purchases were made following his marriage, and one wonders perhaps whether they were made at the instigation of Margaret Williams in an attempt to project her husband and herself into 'county society'? Or were they a gesture on Owen' s part to impress his new wife and parents-in-law? The truth probably lies in an amalgam of these theories, but it is more important to realise that Owen Williams bought these properties, studs and herds at inflationary wartime prices, selling them in 1924 for a fraction of the sum originally paid in a desperate attempt to prop up his ailing shipping enterprise. Had he followed the example of certain shrewd Cardiff shipowners such as W.J. Tatem (who invested much of his wartime profits in government stock), Owen Williams would have had reserves of capital available that might have saved his shipping venture in the mid-1920s.

Such was the scale of the financial crisis that engulfed Owen Williams's business during the 1920s, however, that it is difficult to see how it could have been saved. His mortgage loans to the Lyndon and Brynllwyd shipping firms were injudicious, leading to a loss of over £20,000 in the case of the latter venture alone. The two steamers that remained under his ownership, the MENAPIAN and the MENEVIAN were some twenty years old at the time, and large sums were spent on repairs and on the conversion of both vessels to oil firing. Moreover, the low freight rates that prevailed from late 1920 onwards meant that the vessels incurred a massive loss of over £95,000 on their trading between 1920 and 1925. Owen's attempt to modernise the fleet by the acquisition of motor vessels was original in concept, but he suffered the bad luck that is sometimes the lot of the pioneer who adopts new and only partly-proven technology. The failure of the MARGRETIAN's engines, coinciding as it did with a period of tremendous upheaval in the shipping industry as a result of the slump, dealt Owen Williams a blow from which he, as a shipowner, could never recover. In better times he might have had a chance of recovering his massive outlay of capital, but not in south Wales in the 1920s.

It is tempting, nevertheless, with the benefit of hindsight, to conjecture how Owen Williams's fleet might have developed had the motor vessels proved successful, and had he not been dragged down by financial crisis in the 1920s. Between 1898 and 1912, he and his brother had built up a diverse fleet, comprising smaller steamers that maintained the Golden Cross Line service and larger ocean-going vessels operating in the world-wide tramping trades. Was it perhaps Owen's aim to repeat this pattern in the 1920s, with fast yet modestly-sized cargo liners, similar to the MARGRETIAN, running to the Mediterranean, and substantial motor tramps of comparable size and design to the second SILURIAN trading world-wide? These are admittedly speculative thoughts, but this writer is of the firm opinion that Owen Williams has not received the recognition that he deserves for his role in the development of the motor cargo vessel. The SILURIAN of 1924, especially, was a remarkable pioneering vessel; almost twice the size of the average contemporary tramp and with engines fitted astern, she was a true bulk carrier built over thirty years before such vessels began to supplant the traditional tramp from the late 1950s onwards. In the history of motor shipping and the development of the bulk cargo-carrying vessel, Owen Williams is a prophet without honour in his own land.

Owen and Watkin Williams were the products of one of a number of remarkable communities in north Wales that were, in the nineteenth and early twentieth centuries, capable of producing the managers, labour and a substantial part of the capital needed to establish and operate shipping companies. For many years they operated a highly successful shipping enterprise that was noteworthy for its pioneering aspects. They ran a cargo liner service from one of the foremost tramping ports in the world, and Owen was the first to acquire motor vessels in the globe's foremost coal-exporting port. The venture eventually collapsed in circumstances that were financially disastrous and personally saddening. Nevertheless, the events of 1920-25 should not be allowed to cloud the achievements of two men who rose from quite modest circumstances to be the principals of one of Cardiff's foremost shipping firms. It is most improbable that we will see their like again.

## FLEET LIST NOTES

The notation '1', '2' in brackets after a ship's name denotes that she was the first or second ship of that name in the fleet.

The ship's official number (O.N.) in the British registry is given, followed by her tonnages, gross (g) and net (n) and her dimensions.

Dimensions given are registered length x beam x depth, in feet and tenths.

The types of engine and the names of the engine builders are given; 'C. 2-cyl.' denotes a compound two-cylinder steam engine, 'T. 3-cyl.' denotes a triple expansion three-cylinder steam engine. For motor vessels, the number of cylinders is given and whether they are two stroke cycle (2 S.C.) or four stroke cycle (4 S.C.), and single acting (S.A.).

# FLEET LIST

(I am grateful to Mr. Harold Appleyard, Mr. David Burrell, Mr. Robin Craig, Mr. Rowan Hackman and Mr. Kevin O'Donoghue for their assistance in the compilation of this fleet list.)

**1. HESPERIDES** In the Fleet: **1895-97**
O.N. 87978. 2404g. 1553n. 286.5 x 38.3 x 24.3 feet.
C.2-cyl. by G. Forrester & Co., Liverpool.
13.3.1884: Launched by R. & J. Evans & Co., Liverpool (Yard No. 115), for R.P. Houston & Co., Liverpool, for the transportation of frozen meat from the River Plate. 1895: Purchased by Hesperides Ltd. (O. W. Williams, managers), Cardiff, and later converted to a dry cargo vessel. 10.10.1897: Ran aground on Hatteras Shoal, whilst bound from Santiago de Cuba to Baltimore with a cargo of iron ore and became a constructive total loss.

**2. SILURIAN (1)** In the Fleet: **1898-1914**
O.N. 105200. 940g. 450n. 220.0 x 32.5 x 15.2 feet.
T.3-cyl. by MacColl & Pollock, Sunderland.
4.8.1898: Launched by R. Craggs & Sons, Middlesbrough (Yard No. 145), for the Silurian Steamship Co. Ltd. (O. & W. Williams, managers), Cardiff. 9.1898: Completed. 13.12.1914: Blown ashore at Angerias whilst bound from Cardiff to Oporto with a cargo of coal; the vessel subsequently broke up and was declared a constructive total loss.

The **CANGANIAN** sailing from Swansea on her maiden voyage to Bayonne in February 1900. *(Gwynedd Archives Service, Henry Parry Collection)*

**3. CANGANIAN** In the Fleet: **1900-16**
O.N. 109794. 1143g. 706n. 225.0 x 34.0 x 14.4 feet.
T.3-cyl. by Ross & Duncan, Glasgow.
14.12.1899: Launched by Mackie & Thomson, Glasgow (Yard No. 240), for the Canganian Steamship Co. Ltd. (O. & W. Williams, managers), Cardiff. 2.1900: Completed. 27.12.1916: Reported missing with all hands having sailed from Methil on 17.11.1916 with a cargo of coal for Scapa Flow whilst on service as an Admiralty collier. She had in fact struck a mine off Montrose on 17.11.1916.

DEMETIAN at an Italian port. *(K. J. O'Donoghue collection)*

4. **DEMETIAN** In the Fleet: **1900-20**
O.N. 113527. 1108g. 696n. 225.0 x 34.0 x 14.2 feet
T.3-cyl. by MacColl & Pollock, Sunderland.
28.4.1900: Launched by W. Harkess & Son, Middlesbrough (Yard No. 150) for the S.S. Demetian & Ordovician Co. Ltd. (O. & W. Williams, managers), Cardiff. 6.1900: Completed. 19.1.1920: Sold to A.J. Pope & Co. Ltd., Cardiff. 5.1920: Sold to M.H. Bland & Co. Ltd., Gibraltar and re-named GIBEL GELAHUI. 1925: Sold to E.E. Hadjilias, Syra, Greece and re-named IRIS. 1929: Sold to N. Antoniou, Syra. 1931: Sold to N.A. Zoiopulos, Piraeus, Greece and re-named CHRISTOS Z. 1934: Broken up at Savona, Italy.

The **ORDOVICIAN** at Bristol. *(E. N. Taylor)*

**5. ORDOVICIAN** In the Fleet: **1900-06**
O.N. 113531. 1112g. 701n. 225.4 x 34.1 x 14.3 feet.
T.3-cyl. by MacColl & Pollock, Sunderland.
12.7.1900: Launched by W. Harkess & Son, Middlesbrough (Yard No. 151) for the S.S. Demetian & Ordovician Co. Ltd. (O. & W. Williams, managers), Cardiff. 8.1900: Completed. 6.1.1906: Ran aground at Torres Vedras, Portugal whilst bound from Swansea to Genoa with a cargo of patent fuel and generals, later declared a constructive total loss.


**6. VENEDOTIAN** In the Fleet: **1901-12**
O.N. 113540. 1168g. 734n. 225.0 x 34.2 x 17.7 feet.
T.3-cyl. by MacColl & Pollock, Sunderland.
19.12.1900: Launched by W. Harkess & Son, Middlesbrough (Yard No. 153) for the Venedotian S.S. Co. Ltd. (O. & W. Williams, managers), Cardiff. 2.1901: Completed. 29.11.1912: Sold to Angf. Aktieb. Thule (T. Willerding, manager), Gothenburg, Sweden and re-named ATLE. 8.11.1914: Sank after striking a mine 7 miles S.E. by E. from Cross Sands light vessel whilst bound from London to Gothenburg with general cargo.


**7. SEGONTIAN** In the Fleet: **1901-19**
O.N. 113542. 1171g. 737n. 224.6 x 34.0 x 17.8 feet.
T.3-cyl. by MacColl & Pollock, Sunderland.
3.4.1901: Launched by W. Harkess & Son, Middlesbrough (Yard No. 154) for the Segontian S.S. Co. Ltd. (O. & W. Williams, managers), Cardiff. 5.1901: Completed. 30.9.1909: Collided with the cargo liner TENASSERIM 5089/05 in the Mersey whilst inward bound from Valencia with a cargo of fruit and generals. The SEGONTIAN was beached at Tranmere in a sinking condition, but was later drydocked and repaired. 11.11.1909: Returned to service. 18.12.1919: Sold to Lyndon Shipping Co. Ltd. (Cottle, Roberts & Co., managers), Cardiff. 13.3.1924: Sold to Rederi A/B Iwar (Ohllson, manager), Malmo, Sweden and re-named RIBERSBORG. 1932: Manager became T. Hillerstrom. 29.10.1956: Laid up pending special survey, later re-named BOLMEN. 9.11.1956: Arrived at Ystad to be broken up.


**8. GOIDELIAN** In the Fleet: **1901-05**
O.N. 113548. 1220g. 769n. 225.0 x 35.1 x 17.8 feet.
T.3-cyl. by MacColl & Pollock, Sunderland.
14.8.1901: Launched by W. Harkess & Son, Middlesbrough (Yard No. 155) for the S.S. Goidelian & Coranian Co. Ltd. (O. & W. Williams, managers), Cardiff. 9.1901: Completed. 24.6.1905: Struck a rock and foundered off Sagres, Portugal whilst bound from Gandia to Liverpool with a cargo of fruit and generals. All hands were saved.


**9. CORANIAN** In the Fleet: **1901-07**
O.N. 115364. 1223g. 770n. 225.0 x 35.1 x 17.8 feet.
T.3-cyl. by MacColl & Pollock, Sunderland.
11.10.1901: Launched by W. Harkess & Son, Middlesbrough (Yard No. 156) for the S.S. Goidelian & Coranian Co. Ltd. (O. & W. Williams, managers), Cardiff.

The **CORANIAN** sailing up the Avon. *(City of Bristol Museum)*

11.1901: Completed. 9.1907: Sold to Motala Rederi Aktieb. (C.A. Arvidson, manager), Motala, Sweden and re-named EMIL R. BOMAN. 1918: Manager became E.A. Enhorning, Sundsvall, Sweden. 28.2.1934: Sold to Angfartygs A/B Kjell (H. Jeansson, manager), Sweden and re-named FRIGG. 1952: Sold to Faruk Ardan, Istanbul, Turkey and re-named CENT. 1954: Sold to Arslan Muessesesi, Turkey. 1955: Sold to Huseryin Taviloglu, Turkey and re-named TAVILOGLU. 1958: Sold to Rustu Aldikacti ve Ortagi Donatma Istiraki, Turkey and re-named ILHAN. 1968: Sold to Turkish shipbreakers.

**10. ARVONIAN** In the Fleet: **1905-17**
O.N. 119973. 2794g. 1784n. 331.3 x 47.6 x 20.1 feet.
T.3-cyl. by Blair & Co. Ltd., Stockton-on-Tees.
9.1905: Completed as ARVONIAN by Richardson, Duck & Co. Ltd., Stockton-on-Tees (Yard No. 565) for the S.S. Goidelian & Coranian Co. Ltd. (O. & W. Williams, managers), Cardiff, having been launched 1.8.1905 (as ROSEDALE for the Dale Steamship Co. Ltd. (Lucas & Co., managers), Bristol). 8.10.1913: Transferred to the Venedotian S.S. Co. Ltd. (same managers). 28.8.1917: Requisitioned for use as a 'Q-ship' by the Royal Navy, re-named H.M.S. BENDISH and operated under a series of false names. 20.11.1917: Sold to the Admiralty. 26.11.1917: Transferred to the U.S. Navy and re-named U.S.S. SANTEE. 27.12.1917: Torpedoed by the German submarine U61 whilst sailing from Queenstown to Bantry Bay on a crew-training exercise. Despite serious damage, she was towed to Queenstown by the tug PALADIN and spent five months being repaired. 6.1918: Re-commissioned as H.M.S. BENDISH, and sent to Gibraltar for further 'Q-ship' operations. 3.1919: Sold to James Cadman and re-named ARVONIAN. 7.1919: Sold to the Rhondda Shipping & Coal Exporting Co. Ltd. (Owen & James, managers), Cardiff and 11.1919 re-named BROOKVALE. 1928: Sold to P. Dannebergs, Riga and re-named SPIDOLA. 22.7.1940: Owners became the Latvian Soviet Socialist Republic following the invasion of Latvia by the U.S.S.R. 5.8.1940: Ownership transferred to the U.S.S.R. following the incorporation of Latvia by Russia. 30.6.1941: Seized as a war prize by Germany whilst in dry dock at Liepaja, following the outbreak of war between Germany and Russia. 20.2.1942: Allocated as a supply ship to the German Navy, placed under the management of Schulte & Bruns, Emden and re-named RUDAU. 18.9.1943: Struck a submerged wreck in

The **ARVONIAN**, possibly at Penarth Dock, February 1912.   *(Mr. Alfred Jones, Llanbedrog)*

Greifswald Bay on the German coast, and sustained considerable damage, but was later repaired. 9.10.1944: Attacked by the R.A.F. off the south coast of Norway and was eventually towed to Bergen for repairs. 10.7.1945: Inspected by the Allied Shipping Commission and placed in service as a troop/prisoner of war transport between Norway and Germany. 1946: Laid up at Kiel. 15.4.1947: Taken over by the Ministry of Transport, re-named SPIDOLA and placed under the management of Richard W. Jones & Co., Newport. 14.2.1948: Ran aground on Holy Island, Anglesey due to an extinguished lighthouse whilst homeward bound with a cargo of iron ore from the Mediterranean. 16.2.1948: Refloated and later repaired. 12.1952: Returned to her rightful owner, Mrs. Velta Neimans, the daughter of P. Dannebergs. She was registered under the ownership of Compania P. Dannebergs Ltda., Puerto Limon, Costa Rica and managed by M.Y. McCormick & Co., Universal Shipping Agencies, Liverpool. 1958: Sold to Walter Ritscher, Hamburg and broken up later that year at Harburg.

**11. CYMRIAN** In the Fleet: **1906-17**
O.N. 120493. 1014g. 609n. 215.6 x 32.1 x 15.3 feet.
T.3-cyl. by G.T. Grey, South Shields.
18.11.1904: Launched by A. Vuijk, Capelle a/d Ysel, Holland (Yard No. 253) as KINGWOOD for A. & O. Williams, London. 1.1905: Completed. 4.1906: Purchased by O. & W. Williams, Cardiff and re-named CYMRIAN. 7.1906: Transferred to the Golden Cross Line Ltd. (O. & W. Williams, managers), Cardiff. 25.8.1917: Torpedoed and sunk 13 miles S.S.E. of the Tuskar Rock whilst bound from Newport to Dublin. Ten lives were lost.

**12. MERVINIAN** In the Fleet: **1906-07**
O.N. 99026. 1969g. 1268n. 276.3 x 36.0 x 14.1 feet.
T.3-cyl. by Central Marine Engine Works, West Hartlepool.
20.10.1891: Launched by W. Gray & Co. Ltd., West Hartlepool (Yard No. 430) as SPHEROID for Scrutton, Sons & Co., London. 12.1891: Completed. 1906: Purchased by the Golden Cross Line Ltd. (O. & W. Williams, managers), Cardiff and re-named MERVINIAN. 3.10.1907: Foundered in the Bay of Biscay 100 miles S. of the Scilly Isles whilst bound from Swansea to Marseilles with a cargo of coal and generals. Five lives were lost, including that of the master.

**13. EDERNIAN** In the Fleet: **1906-17**
O.N. 123166. 3588g. 2284n. 342.0 x 51.0 x 22.7 feet.
T.3-cyl. by North Eastern Marine Engineering Co. Ltd. Sunderland.
7.7.1906: Launched by Craig, Taylor & Co. Ltd., Stockton-on-Tees (Yard No. 117) for the SS Demetian & Ordovician Co. Ltd. (O. & W. Williams, managers), Cardiff. 8.1906: Completed. 30.3.1917: Struck a mine in the English Channel, but managed to reach Dieppe for repairs. 20.8.1917: Torpedoed and sunk 6 miles S.E. of Southwold whilst bound from Middlesbrough to Dieppe with a cargo of steel. Fourteen lives were lost. 1936: Part of the cargo was salved.


**14. SNOWDONIAN** In the Fleet: **1907-17**
O.N. 123189. 3870g. 2402n. 360.1 x 51.8 x 22.3 feet.
T.3-cyl. by Blair & Co. Ltd., Stockton-on-Tees.
19.9.1907: Launched by Richardson, Duck & Co. Ltd., Stockton-on-Tees (Yard No. 588) for O. & W. Williams & Co., Cardiff. 10.1907: Completed. 6.10.1913: Transferred to the S.S. Goidelian & Coranian Co. Ltd. (O. & W. Williams & Co., managers), Cardiff. 2.6.1917: Attacked by gunfire by an enemy submarine in the Mediterranean. The SNOWDONIAN succeeded in escaping by making smoke. 31.7.1917: Captured by the German submarine U155 some 245 miles S.E. of the Azores. The crew took to the lifeboats and the vessel was sunk by an explosive charge placed aboard. At the time she was on service as an Admiralty collier, bound with a cargo of coal from Barry to Freetown.


**15. CARDIFFIAN** In the Fleet: **1907-15**
O.N. 118474. 1015g. 610n. 215.6 x 32.1 x 15.3 feet.
T.3-cyl. by G.T. Grey, South Shields.
4.6.1904: Launched by A. Vuijk, Capelle a/d Ysel, Holland (Yard No. 252) as QUEENWOOD for E.S. Holman, London, but 7.1904 completed for the Shipping Agency Ltd. (G.S. Coram, manager), London. 1904: Sold to Heyne & Hessenmuller, Hamburg, Germany. 1906: Sold to the Hillwood Steamship Co. Ltd. (Wilson & Watson, managers), Grangemouth. 1907: Purchased by O. & W. Williams & Co., Cardiff and re-named CARDIFFIAN. 1915: Sold to W. Coombs, Llanelli and re-named AFON LLIEDI. 1920: Transferred to Afon Lliedi Steamship Co. Ltd. (W. Coombs & Sons, managers), Llanelli. 4.1933: Sold to Marittima Ravennate S.A., Ravenna, Italy and re-named RENO. 18.6.1940: Sank off Ancona after striking a mine.


**16. TAVIAN** In the Fleet: **1912-17**
O.N. 135165. 4567g. 2878n. 390.0 x 52.5 x 25.6 feet.
T.3-cyl. by Blair & Co. Ltd., Stockton-on-Tees.
7.11.1912: Launched by Richardson, Duck & Co. Ltd., Stockton-on-Tees (Yard No. 628) for O. & W. Williams & Co., Cardiff. 12.1912: Completed. 1917: Sold to W. & C.T. Jones Steamship Co. Ltd. (W. & C.T. Jones, managers), Cardiff and re-named TONWEN. 1918: Sold to Griffiths, Lewis Steam Navigation Co. Ltd. (J.C. Gould & Co., managers), Cardiff and re-named GRELWEN. 1920: Owners re-styled as Gould Steamships & Industrials Ltd. (same managers). 1925: Sold to the Derwen Shipping Co. Ltd. (D.G. Hall & Co., managers), Cardiff. 1931: Sold to L.J. Goulandris & Bulgaris Bros. (L.J. Goulandris, manager), Piraeus, Greece and re-named KATINA. 1933: Re-named KATINA BULGARIS. 1934: Owners re-styled N.Th. Bulgaris. 8.2.1939: Sunk by collision with the American steamer MEANTICUT 6061/21, 7 miles south of the Humber Light-vessel whilst bound from Hull to Buenos Aires with a cargo of coal.

The **TAVIAN** of 1912, seen here as the Greek-owned **KATINA BULGARIS** approaching Antwerp on 19 September, 1938. *(Captain J. F. Van Puyvelde, Brussels)*


**17. DEVIAN** In the Fleet: **1915-17**
O.N. 136757. 3689g. 2285n. 365.0 x 51.5 x 22.1 feet.
T.3-cyl. by North Eastern Marine Engineering Co. Ltd. Sunderland.
19.10.1914: Launched by J. Priestman & Co. Ltd., Sunderland (Yard No. 249) for O. & W. Williams & Co., Cardiff. 1.1915: Completed. 1917: Sold to W. & C.T. Jones Steamship Co. Ltd. (W. & C.T. Jones, managers), Cardiff and re-named SANWEN. 29.9.1917: Torpedoed and sunk without warning 50 miles E¾N from Cape Bear whilst bound from the Clyde to Naples with a cargo of coal and coke. Two lives were lost.


**18. MENAPIAN** In the Fleet: **1915-25**
O.N. 115847. 2947g. 1872n. 321.0 x 43.2 x 14.7 feet.
T.3-cyl. by the builders.
24.4.1902. Launched by J. Readhead & Sons, South Shields (Yard No. 361) as STATIA for Scrutton, Sons & Co., London. 6.1902: Completed. 1915: Purchased by O. & W. Williams & Co., Cardiff and re-named MENAPIAN. 1925: Sold to the Byron Steamship Co. Ltd. (M. Embiricos, manager), London and re-named LORD BROUGHTON. 1928: Broken up by the Alloa Shipbreaking Co. Ltd. at Rosyth.


**19. MENEVIAN** In the Fleet: **1915-25**
O.N. 115868. 2929g. 1852n. 321.1 x 43.2 x 14.7 feet.
T.3-cyl. by the builders.
10.6.1902: Launched by J. Readhead & Sons, South Shields (Yard No. 362) as SARSTOON for Scrutton, Sons & Co., London. 8.1902: Completed. 1915: Purchased by O. & W. Williams & Co., Cardiff and re-named MENEVIAN. 1925: Sold to the Bristol City Line of Steamships Ltd. (C. Hill & Sons, managers), Bristol and re-named EXETER CITY. 20.1.1933: Abandoned at sea 600 miles off Cape Race in

The **MENEVIAN** in the Avon Gorge. *(E. N. Taylor)*

a position 46.48N., 38.11W. whilst bound from Fowey to Portland (Maine) and Boston with a cargo of china clay. Four crew members were lost, though 22 were rescued and landed at New York. 24.1.1933: Reported partly submerged at 47.16N., 36.40W.

**20. MARGRETIAN (motor vessel)** In the Fleet: **1923-28**
O.N. 147545. 2578g. 1537n. 297.8 x 43.6 x 21.5 feet.
Two 6-cyl. 2 S.C. SA oil engines by Wm. Beardmore & Co. Ltd., Glasgow, driving twin screws. 1930: Replaced with two 6-cyl. 4 S.C. SA oil engines by Maschfbk. Augsburg-Nurnberg A.G., Augsburg, Germany. 1948: Replaced with a 6-cyl. 2 S.C. SA oil engine by General Machinery Corporation, Hamilton, Ohio, U.S.A., driving a single screw.
1923: Launched by C. Hill & Sons Ltd., Bristol (Yard No. 148) for O. & W. Williams & Co., Cardiff. 14.11.1923: Ran trials. 6.1925: Laid up at Cardiff. 11.1928: Sold to Stewart & Esplen Ltd., London and re-named GRESHAM. 1930: Transferred to

The **GRESHAM** (ex-MARGRETIAN) in the Roath Basin, Cardiff in 1937.
*(Welsh Industrial & Maritime Museum)*

58

Gresham Shipping Co. Ltd., London and re-engined. 1933: Laid up at Blyth. 8.1936: Sailed for West Africa, but towed into Lisbon after engine failure. 1937: Sold to Th. Brovig, Farsund, Norway and re-named BALLA. 1948: Re-engined and converted to a single screw. 1961: Sold to Transportacion Maritima Mexicana S.A., Piso, Mexico and re-named GUADALAJARA. 1969: Deleted from *Lloyd's Register,* probably broken up at the time.

**21. SILURIAN (2) (motor vessel)** In the Fleet: **1924-27**
O.N. 148497. 6903g. 4345n. 431.2 x 57.2 x 30.7 feet.
Two 6-cyl. 4 S.C. SA oil engines by Wm. Beardmore & Co. Ltd. Glasgow, driving twin screws.
29.5.1924: Launched by the Blythswood Shipbuilding Co. Ltd., Glasgow, (Yard No. 6) for O. & W. Williams & Co., Cardiff. 30.10.1924: Ran trials. 1927: Sold to Furness, Withy & Co. Ltd., London and re-named CYNTHIANA. 23.6.1928: Wrecked at Cape Mala, Panama Bay whilst bound from Bellingham to Grangemouth with a cargo of timber.

**NOTE:** WAR ISLAND 3143/18. In *Lloyd's Register* 1919-20, this vessel is shown as being owned by Owen & Watkin Williams. Upon completion by Craig, Taylor & Co. Ltd. of Stockton-on-Tees in 1918, she was allocated by the Shipping Controller to Gibbs & Co., Cardiff. On 10 June 1919, she was sold to Watkin J. Williams of Cardiff and re-named COSMOS VOLGA. It would appear that *Lloyd's Register* confused Watkin J. Williams (who later went into partnership with his brother Pardoe Williams to form Williams Bros. (Cardiff) Ltd.) with Watkin Williams, Owen Williams's partner, for the *Lloyd's Confidential Index,* 1920, and the *Service List* of 1921 both show that she was never owned or operated by Owen & Watkin Williams. I am grateful to Mr. David Burrell and Mr. Kevin O'Donoghue for their assistance in sorting out yet another case of confusion involving a common Welsh surname!!

## VESSELS MANAGED ON BEHALF OF THE SHIPPING CONTROLLER 1919-21

**M1. JENNY** In the Fleet: **1919-21**
O.N. 118454. 1868g. 1129n. 280.0 x 38.3 x 18.4 feet.
T.3-cyl. by North Eastern Marine Engineering Co. Ltd., Sunderland.
30.5.1904: Launched by Craig, Taylor & Co. Ltd., Stockton-on-Tees (Yard No. 104) for the Jenny Steamship Co. Ltd. (Van Ysselsteyn & Co., managers), London. 6.1904: Completed. 1905: Transferred to Maats. Stoom. Jenny (same managers), Terneuzen, Holland. 1906: Management transferred to A.C. Lensen. 1914: Sold to Westfalische Transport A.G., Emden, Germany. 1919: Surrendered to Great Britain as a prize, allocated to The Shipping Controller and placed under the management of O. & W. Williams & Co., Cardiff. 1921: Sold to Pentaff Steamship Co. Ltd. (D.P. Barnett & Co., managers), Cardiff and re-named PENTAFF. 1926: Sold to Hwah Tung Steamship Co. Ltd. (L.T. Yung, manager), Shanghai, China, and re-named CHUNG WOO. 1927: Sold to Woo Foong Steamship Co. Ltd., Shanghai. 1935: Owners re-styled as Woo Foong Sing Kee Steamship Co. Ltd. 1936: Sold back to Hwah Tung Steamship Co. Ltd., Shanghai. 12.1941: Lost in an unknown location in the Far East.

**M2. KARL LEONHARDT** In the Fleet: **1919-21**
O.N. 143138. 3129g. 1999n. 302.6 x 45.3 x 18.9 feet.
T.3-cyl. by the builders.
1904: Completed by Akt. Ges. "Neptun", Rostock, Germany (Yard No. 236) as HORNBURG for Dampfschiffs-Reederei Horn, Lubeck, Germany. 1918: Sold to Leonhardt & Blumberg, Hamburg, Germany and re-named KARL LEONHARDT. 1919: Surrendered to Great Britain as a prize, allocated to The Shipping Controller and placed under the management of O. & W. Williams & Co., Cardiff. 1921: Sold to the Greek Government and re-named EFXINOS. 1925: Sold to John D. Chandris, Piraeus, Greece and re-named TONIS CHANDRIS. 10.1.1940: Wrecked near Kirkenes.

The German steamer **SOMMERFELD**, which under her later name of **ROMA** was managed by Owen & Watkin Williams in 1919-21. *(G. J. de Boer)*

**M3. ROMA** In the Fleet: **1919-21**
O.N. 143166. 2606g. 1671n. 319.8 x 38.7 x 22.6 feet.
T.3-cyl. by D. Rowan & Son, Glasgow.
26.9.1889: Launched by C. Connell & Co. Ltd., Glasgow (Yard No. 161) as SOMMERFELD for the Deutsch-Australische D.G., Hamburg, Germany. 12.1889: Completed. 1906: Sold to A.C. de Freitas & Co., Hamburg and re-named ROMA. 1911: Sold to Deutsche Levante-Linie, Hamburg. 21.4.1919: Surrendered to Great Britain as a prize, allocated to The Shipping Controller and placed under the management of O. & W. Williams & Co., Cardiff. 1921: Sold to Emil R. Retzlaff, Stettin, Germany and re-named ERDA. 1931: Sold to Sedina Reederei GmbH, Stettin. 1933: Broken up at Rosyth.

## APPENDICES
1. NOMENCLATURE
2. SHIPPING COMPANIES, 1895-1930
3. SELECTED CREW LISTS
4. SOURCES


## NOMENCLATURE

(I am grateful to my friend Dr. Huw Walters and certain of his colleagues at the National Library of Wales, Aberystwyth, who have identified the origins of some of the more obscure names given to their ships by Owen and Watkin Williams.)

SILURIAN - from 'Silures', the Latin name for the prehistoric inhabitants of south-east Wales.
CANGANIAN - from 'Cangan ap Maig o wehelyth Rhos', an early Welsh nobleman.
DEMETIAN - from 'Demetae', the Latin name for the prehistoric inhabitants of south-west Wales.
ORDOVICIAN - from 'Ordovices', the Latin name for the prehistoric inhabitants of mid Wales.
SEGONTIAN - from 'Segontium' the Latin name given to a Roman fortress on the outskirts of present-day Caernarfon.
CORANIAN - from 'Coraniaid', the Welsh name for a legendary tribe famed for their keen hearing.
GOIDELIAN - from 'Goidel', a Celt from Scotland, Ireland or the Isle of Man (as opposed to Brythonic Celts from Wales, Cornwall and Brittany).
VENEDOTIAN - from 'Venedotia', the Latin name for Gwynedd in north-west Wales.
CYMRIAN - from 'Cymru', the Welsh name for Wales (always pronounced with a hard 'c').
ARVONIAN - from 'Arfon', the Welsh name for the lands extending from the River Ogwen westwards to the River Llyfni in north Wales.
EDERNIAN - from 'Edern', Owen and Watkin Williams' native village on the north coast of the Llŷn Peninsula.
MERVINIAN - from 'Mervinia', the Latin name for Meirionnydd in north Wales.
CARDIFFIAN - from 'Cardiff', capital city of Wales.
SNOWDONIAN - from 'Snowdon', the highest mountain in Wales.
TAVIAN - from 'Tâf', the Welsh name for the River Taff that enters the sea at Cardiff.
DEVIAN - from 'Deva', the Latin name for Chester.
MENAPIAN - from 'Menapii', the Latin name for one of the Celtic tribes that dwelt in the lands between the Seine and the Rhine.
MENEVIAN - from 'Menevia', the Latin name for the cathedral city of St. David's in Dyfed.
MARGRETIAN - named after Owen Williams's wife, Margaret.

| HESPERIDES Ltd. | SILURIAN S.S. Co. Ltd. | CANGANIAN S.S. Co. Ltd. | Steamships DEMETIAN & ORDOVICIAN Ltd. | VENEDOTIAN S.S. Co. Ltd. | Steamships GOIDELIAN & CORANIAN Ltd. | SEGONTIAN S.S. Co. Ltd | GOLDEN CROSS LINE Ltd. | Steamship SNOWDONIAN Ltd. | OWEN & WATKIN WILLIAMS & Co. |
|---|---|---|---|---|---|---|---|---|---|
| 1895-98 | 1898-1917 | 1899-1917 | 1899-1930 | 1900-30 | 1900-30 | 1900-30 | 1906-30 | 1907-18 | |
| HESPERIDES 1895-97 | SILURIAN 1898-1914 | CANGANIAN 1900-16 | DEMETIAN 1900-19 | VENEDOTIAN 1901-12 | GOIDELIAN 1901-05 | SEGONTIAN 1901-19 | MERVINIAN 1906-07 | Never vested with the ownership of the SNOWDONIAN | SNOWDONIAN 1907-13 |
| | 20/64th DEVIAN 1915-17 | | ORDOVICIAN 1900-06 | ARVONIAN 1913-17 | CORANIAN 1901-07 | 11/64th MENAPIAN 1915-25 | CYMRIAN 1906-17 | | CARDIFFIAN 1907-15 |
| | | | EDERNIAN 1906-17 | 12/64th MENAPIAN 1915-25 | ARVONIAN 1905-13 | 11/64th MENEVIAN 1915-25 | | | TAVIAN 1912-17 |
| | | | 1/64th MENAPIAN 1915-25 | 12/64th MENEVIAN 1915-25 | SNOWDONIAN 1913-17 | 10/64th MARGRETIAN 1923-28 | | | 44/64th DEVIAN 1915-17 |
| | | | 1/64th MENEVIAN 1915-25 | 5/64th MARGRETIAN 1923-28 | 20/64th MENAPIAN 1915-25 | | | | 20/64th MENAPIAN 1915-25 |
| | | | | | 20/64th MENEVIAN 1915-25 | | | | 20/64th MENEVIAN 1915-25 |
| | | | | | 17/64th MARGRETIAN 1923-28 | | | | 32/64th MARGRETIAN 1923-28 |
| | | | | | | | | | SILURIAN (2) 1924-27 |

**OWEN AND WATKIN WILLIAMS:
SHIPPING COMPANIES
1895-1930**

## SELECTED CREW LISTS
(Taken from the archive of the Maritime History Group of the Memorial University of St. John's, Newfoundland, Canada.)

Crew of **TAVIAN**
Signed-on at Cardiff, 18 June 1913

|  | aged |
|---|---|
| J. D. Griffith, Edern, master | 38 |
| E. Jones, Aberaeron, 1st mate | 34 |
| W. Humphreys, Barry, 2nd mate | 47 |
| W. Jones, Brynsiencyn, steward | 34 |
| P. Farrier, London, cook | 25 |
| W. H. Williams, Brynsiencyn, master's steward | 35 |
| C. Truman, Cardiff, assistant cook and cabin boy | 15 |
| D. Williams, Pwllheli, carpenter | 20 |
| D. Owen, Conwy, bosun | 39 |
| D. Jones, Nefyn, A.B. | 39 |
| R. Roberts, Abersoch, A.B. | 21 |
| J. Larrey, Appledore, O.S. | 20 |
| E. G. Thomas, Aberaeron, O.S. | 20 |
| E. T. Jones, Llangrannog, A.B. | 23 |
| J. W. Johansenn, Cardiff (Swedish), O.S. | 28 |
| J. Roberts, Edern, O.S. | 16 |
| W. T. Davies, Neath, 1st engineer | 45 |
| T. D. Rees, Swansea, 2nd engineer | 43 |
| R. Goodsire, Musselburgh, 3rd engineer | 52 |
| J. Wright, Stockton, 4th engineer | 22 |
| C. Baines, Middlesbrough, donkeyman | 44 |
| J. Bradley, Hull, fireman | 26 |
| J. Bard, Malta, fireman | 29 |
| A. Gasan, Malta, fireman | 30 |
| A. Manning, Cork, fireman | 35 |
| C. Scotino, Malta, fireman | 23 |
| T. Alund, Cardiff (Finnish), fireman | 19 |
| D. Roberts, Bryncroes, fireman | 28 |
| J. Logan, Belfast, fireman | 28 |
| A. Elton, Nottingham, fireman | 30 |
| B. Hayer, Cardiff (German), fireman | 40 |
| L. Brimer, Cardiff, apprentice | 21 |
| H. Davies, Nefyn, apprentice | 16 |
| E. Williams, Rhostryfan, apprentice | 17 |
| L. T. Lewis, Cardiff, apprentice | 17 |
| T. L. Ellis, Pwllheli, apprentice | 17 |

Crew of **CARDIFFIAN**
Signed-on at Cardiff, 3 July 1913

| | aged |
|---|---|
| C.S. Whyatt, Swansea, master | 42 |
| W.C. Roberts, Nefyn, mate | 25 |
| Daniel Jones, Llangrannog, bosun | 43 |
| David Villa, Malta, cook and steward | 27 |
| C.A. Lewis, Brecon, master's steward | 17 |
| T.J. Owen, Llangrannog, A.B. | 20 |
| B. Balmain, Glasgow, A.B. | 21 |
| Gabriel Jones, Clynnog Fawr, A.B. | 21 |
| A.C. Culver, Canterbury, A.B. | 26 |
| D. Morris, Cardigan, O.S. | 19 |
| S. Thomas, Cardiff, O.S. | 15 |
| R. Edwards, Llangefni, 1st engineer | 41 |
| S. Burcombe, Bristol, 2nd engineer | 32 |
| E. Augusto, Oporto, donkeyman | 32 |
| P. Vanderbeen, Antwerp, fireman | 27 |
| J. Fontanalis, Barcelona, fireman | 31 |
| G. Garcioma, Malta, fireman | 33 |


Crew of **SNOWDONIAN**
Signed-on at Hamburg, 22 November 1913

| | aged |
|---|---|
| G. Roberts, Edern, master | 43 |
| J. E. Evans, Llanon, 1st mate | 28 |
| O. D. Griffiths, Port Dinorwig, 2nd mate | 37 |
| E. R. Lewis, St. Dogmaels, steward | 38 |
| T. McGee, Middlesbrough, cook | 24 |
| A. Ralind, Copenhagen, carpenter | 48 |
| P. Janson, Malmo, bosun | 38 |
| C. Burnham, Georgetown, Guyana, A.B. | 22 |
| P. Rytter, Copenhagen, A.B. | 24 |
| Y. Pedersen, Copenhagen, A.B. | 24 |
| H. C. Moller, Hamburg, A.B. | 20 |
| N. Damkjar, Copenhagen, A.B. | 29 |
| H. Christian, Ramsgate, O.S. | 26 |
| Ll. Griffith, Bangor, 1st engineer | 47 |
| S. R. Tuckfield, Swansea, 2nd engineer | 48 |
| J. R. Sims, Liverpool, 3rd engineer | 31 |
| R. McLeod, Barrow, 4th engineer | 23 |
| H. Williams, Nefyn, donkeyman | 43 |
| E. Bietermann, Hamburg, fireman | 49 |
| W. Feddern, Hamburg, fireman | 31 |
| M. Lenz, Hamburg, fireman | 48 |
| D. Moberg, Helsingborg, fireman | 23 |
| D. Ramon, Valparaiso, fireman | 29 |
| S. Spitsy, Freiburg, fireman | 38 |
| A. Corelt, Copenhagen, fireman | 42 |

| | |
|---|---|
| W. H. Miles, Cadoxton, apprentice | 20 |
| H. P. Roberts, Port Dinorwig, apprentice | 19 |
| E. J. Thomas, Cardiff, apprentice | 19 |
| R. L. Williams, Rhostryfan, apprentice | 18 |

Crew of **DEMETIAN**
Signed-on at Bristol, 5 January 1914

| | aged |
|---|---|
| J. Herbert, Nefyn, master | 46 |
| J. Evans, Caernarfon, mate | 54 |
| T. Davies, Llanarth, bosun | 42 |
| G. Evans, Morfa Nefyn, cook and steward | 48 |
| D. Paté, Cape Verde Islands, A.B. | 50 |
| D. Lewis, Borth, A.B. | 22 |
| E. Rees, Llangennydd, A.B. | 32 |
| R. H. Williams, Nefyn, O.S. | 17 |
| T. P. Morris, Borth, O.S. | 22 |
| D. Pritchard, Swansea, O.S. | 18 |
| T. Jones, Edern, O.S. | 17 |
| T. Williams, Benllech, 1st engineer | 30 |
| F. G. Bruce, Lerwick, 2nd engineer | 58 |
| J. Fernandez, Bristol (Spanish), donkeyman | 26 |
| J. R. Hughes, Nefyn, fireman | 29 |
| T. Gomez, Bristol (Spanish), fireman | 21 |
| J. Lang, Kirkcaldy, fireman | 25 |

Crew of **CANGANIAN**
Signed-on at Swansea, 16 February 1914

| | aged |
|---|---|
| Hugh Roberts, Edern, master | 39 |
| E.H. Williams, Porthmadog, mate | 41 |
| William Thomas, Morfa Nefyn, bosun | 46 |
| Evan Jones, Aberystwyth, cook and steward | 56 |
| Evan Roberts, Porthdinllaen, A.B. | 26 |
| H. Padesta, Swansea (Spanish), A.B. | 55 |
| M. Williams, Benllech, A.B. | 26 |
| Joseph Plunkett, Swansea, A.B. | 26 |
| G.T. Williams, Edern, O.S. | 17 |
| Ellis Jones, Edern, O.S. | 15 |
| Edwin Jones, Penrhyndeudraeth, 1st engineer | 32 |
| Thomas Jenkins, Abercych, 2nd engineer | 40 |
| G. Ambrose, Swansea (Ceylon), donkeyman | 24 |
| Edgar Forbes, Swansea (Jamaican), fireman | 22 |
| John Foster, Swansea (Jamaican), fireman | 37 |
| Luther Osborne, Swansea (Jamaican), fireman | 23 |

Crew of **EDERNIAN**
Signed-on at Barry, 28 April 1914

| | aged |
|---|---|
| D. Alban Thomas, Aberaeron, master | 35 |
| W. Griffith, Nefyn, 1st mate | 45 |
| Ll. Owen, Llanbedrog, 2nd mate | 20 |
| D. Jones, Aberaeron, bosun | 41 |
| L. G. Lewis, Aberaeron, carpenter | 22 |
| H. Roberts, Edern, O.S. | 18 |
| E. Ward, Cardiff, O.S. | 18 |
| R. Williams, Edern, A.B. | 19 |
| D. Evans, Aberaeron, A.B. | 19 |
| R. O. Griffiths, Nefyn, O.S. | 17 |
| E. Griffiths, Pwllheli, 1st engineer | 41 |
| T. Evans, Caernarfon, 2nd engineer | 51 |
| J. R. Sanderson, Gateshead, 3rd engineer | 28 |
| F. Nairn, Dublin, 4th engineer | 22 |
| J. Hakanson, Cardiff (Swedish), donkeyman | 23 |
| J. Dobson, Pwllheli, fireman | 33 |
| E. Noon, Hull, fireman | 34 |
| S. Collins, Southampton, fireman | 21 |
| A. Bearman, Portsmouth, fireman | 45 |
| J. Simpson, Nelson, fireman | 24 |
| J. Gillick, Plymouth, fireman | 34 |
| K. Suomi, Cardiff (Finnish), fireman | 24 |
| F. Silva, Cardiff (Spanish), fireman | 27 |
| T. J. Williams, Pwllheli, steward | 34 |
| D. J. Griffiths, Nefyn, master's steward | 15 |
| J. Villa, Malta, cook | 59 |
| W. G. James, Aberdare, apprentice | 21 |
| N. J. Robson, London, apprentice | 18 |


Crew of **CYMRIAN**
Signed-on at Liverpool, 22 July 1914

| | aged |
|---|---|
| J.R. Jones, Llangrannog, master | 30 |
| H. Jones, Criccieth, mate | 42 |
| John Hughes, Pwllheli, bosun | 54 |
| H. Robinson, Philadelphia, cook and steward | 38 |
| P.J. McCafferty, Belfast, master's steward | 16 |
| W. Bowen, Moylgrove, A.B. | 20 |
| J. Thomas, Llangrannog, A.B. | 43 |
| E.J. Roberts, Aberdaron, A.B. | 38 |
| F. Verdigo, Liverpool (Spanish), O.S. | 20 |
| E.T. Phillips, Aberporth, O.S. | 16 |
| W.J. Abrahams, Cardiff, 1st engineer | 34 |
| W. McDermid, Oswestry, 2nd engineer | 41 |
| S. Ahmed, Aden, donkeyman | 37 |

| | |
|---|---|
| A. Ali, Aden, fireman | 34 |
| M. Ahmed, Aden, fireman | 27 |
| A. Sharif, Aden, fireman | 38 |
| A. Farr, Cardiff, apprentice | 19 |

Crew of **MENAPIAN**
Signed-on at Bristol, 30 October 1923

| | aged |
|---|---|
| H. Roberts, Edern, master | 49 |
| G. Jones, Caernarfon, 1st mate | 50 |
| W. Roberts, Amlwch, 2nd mate | 25 |
| R. T. Jones, Nefyn, 3rd mate | 51 |
| H. C. Griffiths, Brynsiencyn, bosun | 24 |
| W. E. Jones, Tudweiliog, A.B. | 26 |
| D. R. Jones, Porthmadog, A.B. | 26 |
| T. Jones, Nefyn, A.B. | 23 |
| W. R. Owen, Edern, O.S. | 20 |
| W. Roberts, Edern, O.S. | 20 |
| E. Owen, Edern, O.S. | 19 |
| R. Owen, Edern, O.S. | 17 |
| E. Jones, Porthmadog, 1st engineer | 49 |
| A. J. Slater, Bristol, 2nd engineer | 49 |
| F. W. Tanner, Bristol, 3rd engineer | 23 |
| J. Hughes, Caernarfon, donkeyman | 48 |
| J. H. Somers, Bristol, fireman | 31 |
| G. Thornby, Bristol, fireman | 30 |
| J. McIntyre, Bristol, fireman | 42 |
| G. Olsen, Bristol (Danish), fireman | 55 |
| S. Alford, Bristol, fireman | 40 |
| D. J. O'Keeffe, Cork, fireman | 36 |
| A. Kayser, London, fireman | 30 |
| J. Roberts, Nefyn, steward | 46 |
| H. Jones, Tudweiliog, assistant steward | 26 |
| W. Spiers, Paisley, cook | 47 |
| H. H. Dunn, London, wireless operator | 24 |
| J. E. Watts, Swansea, apprentice | 16 |
| W. J. Davies, Cardiff, apprentice | 17 |

Crew of **MARGRETIAN**
Signed-on at Bristol, 1 November 1923

| | aged |
|---|---|
| D. J. Jones, Swansea, master | 53 |
| E. T. Tippett, Pill, 1st mate | 44 |
| R. Burn, North Shields, 2nd mate | 32 |
| G. B. Davies, Manordeilo, 3rd mate | 19 |
| R. I. Jones, Liverpool, bosun | 49 |

| | |
|---|---|
| T. Hughes, Porthmadog, A.B. | 21 |
| A. Beard, Birmingham, A.B. | 32 |
| E. Pullin, Bristol, A.B. | 21 |
| A. Pocock, Bristol, A.B. | 26 |
| L. Davies, Bristol, A.B. | 58 |
| C. Kenwood, Swansea, O.S. | 16 |
| E. Griffiths, Pwllheli, 1st engineer | 52 |
| M. J. Mellinton, Sunderland, 2nd engineer | 31 |
| G. Bell, Leeds, 3rd engineer | 27 |
| C. J. Moon, Cardiff, 4th engineer | 31 |
| W. C. North, London, donkeyman | 40 |
| W. Chaffy, Swindon, greaser | 38 |
| G. H. Pocock, Bristol, greaser | 34 |
| G. Griffiths, Pwllheli, greaser | 25 |
| C. Thomas, Gloucester, steward | 48 |
| C. Cheetah, Exmouth, cook | 55 |
| G. W. Garratt, Bristol, master's steward | 19 |
| W. E. Warren, Bristol, wireless operator | 22 |
| T. P. Davison, Maryport, 'guarantee engineer' (Maiden voyage) | 32 |

Crew of **MENEVIAN**
Signed-on at Bristol, 27 December 1923

| | aged |
|---|---|
| G. Roberts, Edern, master | 52 |
| J. E. Evans, Llanon, 1st mate | 38 |
| I. Williams, Abersoch, 2nd mate | 36 |
| J. Thomas, Nefyn, 3rd mate | 51 |
| W. Davies, Pistyll, bosun | 23 |
| M. Leonard, Dublin, A.B. | 30 |
| R. Roberts, Aberdaron, A.B. | 23 |
| W. Smith, Bristol, A.B. | 22 |
| W. Stuckey, Bristol, A.B. | 23 |
| J. H. Evans, Edern, O.S. | 22 |
| R. O. Jones, Edern, O.S. | 20 |
| J. Thomas, Cardiff, 1st engineer | 53 |
| L. B. Tucker, Cardiff, 2nd engineer | 27 |
| J. Medlands, London, 3rd engineer | 46 |
| A. C. Evans, Cowbridge, 4th engineer | 21 |
| J. R. Hughes, Nefyn, donkeyman | 39 |
| F. Smith, Bristol, fireman | 37 |
| J. McKeough, Portadown, fireman | 36 |
| P. McGrath, Plymouth, fireman | 56 |
| J. E. Evans, Llanon, steward | 39 |
| D. J. Evans, Nefyn, cook | 57 |
| R. H. Hughes, Edern, master's steward | 21 |
| T. C. Maycock, London, wireless operator | 31 |
| E. P. Richards, Cardiff, apprentice | 19 |
| L. C. Thomas, Cheltenham, apprentice | 19 |
| H. Hughes, Talysarn, apprentice | 16 |

## SOURCES
(This is not intended to be a comprehensive bibliography, but a simple guide to the chief sources consulted.)

*1. Documentary Sources*
Crew Lists - Maritime History Archive, Memorial University of Newfoundland, St. John's, Newfoundland, Canada.
Defunct Companies Files - Public Record Office, Kew, London.
Lloyd's Captains Registers - Guildhall Library, London.
Official Inquiries into Shipping Losses - Department of Transport, Marine Library, Sunley House, High Holborn, London.
Report on the Salvage of the SEGONTIAN - Welsh Industrial and Maritime Museum, Cardiff.
Shipping Registers, Port of Cardiff - Glamorgan Archive Service and H.M. Customs & Excise, Cardiff.

*2. Newspapers and Journals*
Caernarfon & Denbigh Herald
Cardiff & South Wales Journal of Commerce
Lloyd's List
Maritime Review
South Wales Daily News
The Motor Ship
Western Mail

*3. Printed Books*
British Vessels Lost at Sea, 1914-1918 (H.M.S.O., 1919).
Lloyd's Registers
J. E. Cowden & J.O.C. Duffy, The Elder Dempster Fleet History 1852-1985 (1986).
Robin Craig, Steam Tramps and Cargo Liners 1850-1950 (1980).
D. E. Fayle, The War and the Shipping Industry (1927).
A. C. Hardy, History of Motorshipping (1955).
Paul Heaton, Welsh Blockade Runners in the Spanish Civil War (1985).
Carson I. Ritchie, Q-ships (1985).
Iona Roberts, Hen Luniau Edern a Phorthdinllaen 2 (1989).

*4. Articles*
J. L. Loughran, 'More Charter Markings', Sea Breezes, Vol. 48, No. 343, July 1974.
D. J. Morgan, 'Boom and Slump - Shipowning at Cardiff 1919-21', Maritime Wales No.12, 1989.
Ben Bowen Thomas, 'The schooner Mary Watkins', Transactions of the Caernarfonshire Historical Society, Vol.4, 1942-43.

# INDEX OF SHIPS' NAMES

The number refers to the entry in the fleet list. Names in capitals are those carried under ownership or management; other previous or subsequent names are given in lower case letters.

| | | | |
|---|---|---|---|
| Afon Lliedi | 15 | ,Katina | 16 |
| ARVONIAN | 10 | Katina Bulgaris | 16 |
| Atle | 6 | Kingwood | 11 |
| Balla | 20 | Lord Broughton | 18 |
| H.M.S. Bendish | 10 | MARGRETIAN | 20 |
| Bolmen | 7 | MENAPIAN | 18 |
| Brookvale | 10 | MENEVIAN | 19 |
| CANGANIAN | 3 | MERVINIAN | 12 |
| CARDIFFIAN | 15 | ORDOVICIAN | 5 |
| Cent | 9 | Pentaff | M1 |
| Christos Z | 4 | Queenwood | 15 |
| Chung Woo | M1 | Reno | 15 |
| CORANIAN | 9 | Ribersborg | 7 |
| CYMRIAN | 11 | ROMA | M3 |
| Cynthiana | 21 | Rudau | 10 |
| DEMETIAN | 4 | U.S.S. Santee | 10 |
| DEVIAN | 17 | Sanwen | 17 |
| EDERNIAN | 13 | Sarstoon | 19 |
| Efxinos | M2 | SEGONTIAN | 7 |
| Emil R. Boman | 9 | SILURIAN (1) | 2 |
| Erda | M3 | SILURIAN (2) | 21 |
| Frigg | 9 | Sommerfeld | M3 |
| Gibel Gelahui | 4 | SNOWDONIAN | 14 |
| GOIDELIAN | 8 | Spheroid | 12 |
| Grelwen | 16 | Spidola | 10 |
| Gresham | 20 | Statia | 18 |
| Guadalajara | 20 | TAVIAN | 16 |
| HESPERIDES | 1 | Taviloglu | 9 |
| Hornburg | M2 | Tonis Chandris | M2 |
| Ilhan | 9 | Tonwen | 16 |
| Iris | 4 | VENEDOTIAN | 6 |
| JENNY | M1 | | |
| KARL LEONHARDT | | | |
| | M2 | | |

## ITALY, MARSEILLES AND SPAIN.

*DIRECT SERVICE between*
Liverpool, Bristol, Swansea and Genoa, Leghorn, Marseilles, Tarragona, Valencia, &c., and *vice versa.*

# GOLDEN CROSS LINE.

*For Freight, &c., apply to the Owners:—*
OWEN & WATKIN WILLIAMS & CO.,
BALTIC HOUSE - - - CARDIFF.

Telegraphic Address: "CHARTER," Cardiff.
Telephone: 3074, 3075.

# WORLD SHIP SOCIETY PUBLICATIONS

This is one of a substantial number of shipping company histories published by the World Ship Society. Full details are available from the Society at 52 Nursery Road, Sunderland SR3 1NT. Titles in print in 1991 include:

ALBYN LINE
AUSTRALIAN NATIONAL LINE
BLAND GIBRALTAR
CAMBRIAN COASTERS
CHAPMAN OF NEWCASTLE
CONSTANTINE GROUP
CONVERSION FOR WAR
CUNARD PORTRAITS
THE DEN LINE (BARRIE & NAIRN)
DONALDSON LINE*
EMPIRE TUGS
EVERARD OF GREENHITHE*
FERRY MALTA
FROM AMERICA TO UNITED STATES
　In Four Parts
GAS AND ELECTRICITY COLLIERS
GEORGE GIBSON & CO.
THE GORTHON SHIPPING COMPANIES 1915-1985
HAIN OF ST. IVES
HAMBURG SOUTH AMERICA LINE*
HAMBURG TUGS
HEAD LINE (THE ULSTER STEAMSHIP CO. LTD.)
IDYLL OF THE KINGS (KING LINE)
IRISH SHIPPING LTD.
P&O, A FLEET HISTORY*
SCOTTISH FISHERY PROTECTION
SCRAP AND BUILD
SOVIET PASSENGER SHIPS 1917-1977
WM. SLOAN & CO. LTD. 1825-1968
STAG LINE
STEPHENS, SUTTON LTD.
WEST HARTLEPOOL STEAM NAVIGATION CO. LTD.

*Naval Titles:*
HUNT CLASS DESTROYERS
IRISH NAVAL SERVICE
LEANDER CLASS FRIGATES
REGISTER OF TYPE VII U-BOATS
THE TYPE 35 TORPEDO BOATS OF THE KRIEGSMARINE
TOWN CLASS DESTROYERS

　　　　　　　　　　　　　　　*indicates case-bound